Real New Mexico Chile

An Insider's Guide to Cooking With Chile

by
Sandy Szwarc

GOLDEN
WEST ☼
PUBLISHERS

Cover by Patrick J. Szwarc, Rising Sun Design

Acknowledgements

Thank you with all of my heart to three very special people in my life — my husband Patrick, sister Diana Driscoll, and dear friend Lisa Mitchell. Your constant love, support and encouragement have nurtured my soul and career.

Library of Congress Cataloging-in-Publication Data

Szwarc, Sandy
  Real New Mexico Chile / by Sandy Szwarc
     p.   cm.
  Includes index.
  1. Cookery (Peppers)   2. Cookery, American—South-
     western style.   3. Cookery—New Mexico.   I. Title.
  TX803.P46S99   1996   96-1767
  641.6'384—dc20   CIP

Printed in the United States of America

Third Printing ©1998

ISBN #1-885590-15-6

Golden West Publishers, Inc.
4113 N. Longview Ave.
Phoenix, AZ 85014, USA
(602) 265-4392

Contents

Contents (continued on next page)

Contents (continued)

Contents (continued)

INSIDER'S INFORMATION

To have any hope of passing for a native New Mexican, you'll need to learn the lingo. The chile lingo, that is. Otherwise, you'll give away your cover! Requests for chipotle salsa, habanero sauce or a bowl of chuckwagon "chili" with beans will be met with polite smiles and secret chuckles. Red-faced, you'll know you've been labeled a "gringo." To save you from this fate, here's your insider's guide to real New Mexico chile peppers.

The first rule is spelling. It's Chile. Here in New Mexico, it's spelled with an "e" on the end, from the old Spanish spelling. Chile refers both to our chile peppers and the sauces made with our peppers. "Chili," spelled with an "i" refers to that totally different spicy Texas dish with meat, tomatoes and beans.

You've probably already guessed this; New Mexicans are pretty passionate about their chile peppers. With good reason! Our chiles are very different from those found anywhere else in the world. They're unique even throughout the Southwest, including Mexico, California, Arizona and Texas. Although all types of chile peppers are grown here, the favorite of natives, and what we mean when we say "chile," is the New Mexico chile pepper. This type is large, 6 to 7 inches long, with a distinctively robust and earthy flavor. Many varieties can be found within the New Mexico breed - Big Jims, Sandias, Anaheims, Espanolas - and everyone has their favorite. The merits of various peppers are hotly debated in New Mexico, much like vintages of fine wines. You may be surprised to learn that these debates are justified. The taste of a chile will vary not only by the type, but the soil and climate where it's grown, and even the year it's harvested.

Chile peppers have been grown in New Mexico for thousands of years. More continue to be harvested here than in any other state. The main production areas are in the dry valleys of the Rio Grande River in the southern part of the state and in the cooler regions of the north. The heart of the largest chile-growing area is from Hatch to Las Cruces in the south, where over 30,000 acres are cultivated. This region produces thick-fleshed chiles that are usually picked while they're green and then roasted and peeled before being eaten. The smaller growing area around Chimayo, north of Santa Fe, produces generally smaller thinner-fleshed chiles which are often hotter. These chiles are frequently allowed to ripen on the plants further until they become red and are then dried. Hence, the terms red and green chile used by natives.

New Mexicans are uniquely obsessed about chiles. We consume more chiles per capita than residents of any other state! We are said to be addicted to them! Most native residents need a regular "chile-fix." No, this isn't a figment of our imaginations. Actually, a substance found in chiles called capsaicin, has been found to stimulate the body's production of endorphins which might explain their addictiveness.

It's the capsaicin which also gives chiles their hotness. Capsaicin is concentrated around the stems, inner membranes and seeds. The flavor and hotness of green chiles ranges from almost sweet to painfully hot, depending upon which of hundreds of varieties are grown as well as where they're grown. The general rule of thumb is the smaller the chile pepper variety, the hotter it is.

The Scoville test was developed in 1902 to measure the hotness of peppers by dilutability. This scale is now computerized and ranges from zero for bell peppers to 200,000 for the hottest habanero peppers. A simplified rating scale based on the Scoville test, with scores ranging from zero to ten, is also often used.

New Mexico chiles generally fall between 3 and 6 on this scale, but some are far hotter. Never assume that red is hotter than green, or vice versa. Always ask! Hotness is unpredictable, even within varieties. Where the chiles were grown, as well as the temperatures and rainfall during the growing season, all play a role. Years and areas of dry hot weather often make even the mildest varieties hotter. Old New Mexicans have their own theory, though. They believe that the mood of the farmer will determine the chiles' hotness. So, an angry farmer will grow fiery hot chiles!

Chile peppers are the soul of each and every native New Mexican. They have played a long and vital role in our state's history. Traditionally, they've been valued for their ability to help preserve meat due to their antioxidant content. They've been an important folk remedy here, too, being used to soothe the pain of arthritis and ulcers. But, the full range of their long appreciated health benefits has finally been recognized by modern science. Green chiles supply up to six times more vitamin C than oranges and the vitamin content increases as the season advances. They are also high in vitamins A and B. Red chiles have an even higher beta carotene content than green. Chiles have also been found to dilate the blood vessels, thus cooling the body and lowering the blood pressure. It's no wonder that hot and spicy chiles are often the most loved wherever the climate is hot.

During the September and October harvest period, the sharp smokey aroma of roasting green chiles fills neighborhoods throughout our state. It serves almost as a call to action for chile lovers. Farmers' trailers filled with large burlap bags of fresh green chiles can be found at every major street corner. Local produce markets are also in good supply. When purchasing chiles, aficionados select only firm, crisp peppers without wrinkled surfaces or soft spots. The peppers will also have a shiny green color and fresh smell. The chiles that are heavy for their size are prized for having the most flesh. The chile most noted for its thick flesh, perfect for stuffing and using in the popular dish called "chile rellenos," is the Big Jim variety.

The preparation of fresh green chiles is easy. First, they need to be roasted. Traditionally, they are roasted over grills until the outsides are blackened and blistered. But, native New Mexicans usually buy one or two 40-pound sacks each fall for their year's supply. This makes roasting them individually a daunting prospect. So, nowadays, savvy chile lovers take advantage of the large metal cages that revolve over gas flames and, in the hands of a competent roaster, will perfectly roast an entire bag in five minutes. After roasting, the charred chiles are placed in plastic bags which makes them sweat as they cool, loosening the peels.

After they have cooled, the fun begins. As a precaution from burning the skin, eyes and mucous membranes from the acid in the chiles, rubber gloves are worn. Or, before handling the roasted chiles, many natives simply rub their hands with grease or shortening. Then, the chiles' skins are slipped off and the stems removed. Depending on the hotness desired, the inner fibers and seeds may either be kept or discarded. However, chile lovers never rinse chiles in water lest they remove the tasty oils.

Freezing is the best way to preserve the roasted and peeled green chiles not used immediately. They will keep frozen for up to a year.

Because freezing disperses the capsaicin throughout the chile, frozen chiles will be perceived as hotter the longer they are frozen, so watch out!

Some peppers are left on the plant until they turn red. They are then strung together to form bundles, called "ristras," and hung outside to dry. When traveling across the state, you'll frequently spot ristras hanging from vigas in front of homes. Once dried, these red chiles can be used whenever needed throughout the year to make red chile sauce. Dried red chiles that have aged until they've darkened to a brown color will have lost much of their rich flavors. So, like discerning natives, look for the most vividly colored chile ristras and dried chiles when purchasing them.

Dried red chiles may also be crushed to flakes or ground to a powder for use in cooking. Dried chile pepper flakes are often sold in stores labeled as "caribe." By coarsely crushing your own whole dried red chiles, you can make caribe at home that will have more chile flavor and fewer seeds than store bought versions. In New Mexican recipes, "chile powder" refers to pure ground dried chile peppers, not the spice mixtures often labeled "chili powder" in stores elsewhere across the nation.

Traditional New Mexican recipes are simple and wholesome, blending the cuisines of the native American Indians and the Spanish settlers that occupied our state for centuries. Modest ingredients indigenous to

our state such as pinto beans, squashes and corn, form the basis of most dishes. And, of course, chiles dominate the traditional recipes that are still loved today. As the official vegetable of our state, chiles are making their way into modern recipes in a variety of exciting new ways, too. But, most native New Mexicans stick rather close to the simpler origins of our cuisine.

In this book, you'll find my chile recipes which offer creative contemporary New Mexican cooking that still manages to capture the historic roots of our native cuisine. These homestyle recipes are easy to prepare and use a minimum of local ingredients that are readily available. Most are also attentive to current concerns for more healthful eating. Whether you're new to our state or a native yourself, you'll enjoy these new chile recipes as well as the updated versions of your old favorites.

Before you begin cooking, remember that cooking with chiles is an inexact science. Precisely how much chile to use in a recipe should depend on the hotness of your specific chiles and on your own tastes. The measurements given here are for chiles of medium to mild hotness and for local taste buds. They've been repeatedly tested and have won the approval of real New Mexicans. But, don't hesitate to adjust the measurements to your particular situation. If you're new to chiles, start out with lesser quantities and taste the dish before adding the full amount called for. The same goes with the portions given for garlic, onion, salt, etc. For those of you with cast-iron gullets, you may even find these recipes on the tame side!

Second only to chiles, tortillas are a necessary staple of New Mexican cooks. Tortillas are thin circles of a skillet-baked dough made of corn or leavened wheat flour. Corn tortillas are essential for making enchiladas and nachos. Flour tortillas are the bread of New Mexican meals and are often served as accompaniments to the main dish. They are also required for making burritos and tostadas.

The earliest tortillas were made by ancient Pueblo Indians from dried corn that was ground with the ashes from burned desert plants. This meal was then mixed with water to make a stiff dough, patted flat with the palm of the hand, and cooked on heated rocks until puffed and lightly golden. Nowadays, most New Mexicans purchase factory-made corn tortillas. They are widely available here, fresh or frozen, and most agree they are comparable to homemade. Making corn tortillas at home is a time-consuming challenge for even the most experienced cook. If you want to attempt them, the most readily available mix is "Masa Harina." Just follow the directions. Corn tortillas are about 6-inches across.

Flour tortillas are twice as large and are usually made thicker and fluffier than corn. Although plenty of commercially-made flour tortillas are always locally available to New Mexicans, there is no denying that those made at home and served fresh off the griddle are the best. They are relatively simple to prepare using ingredients stocked in most kitchens. They do, however, require some time and are best when made at the last minute. (See my version for homemade tortillas on page 36.)

Real New Mexico Chile

THE BASICS

Traditional-Style New Mexico Green Chile Sauce

A good green chile sauce is the cornerstone for every real New Mexican cook. Culinary reputations stand or fall on one's chile sauce alone. Chile sauces may be served at any meal. At breakfast, it's spooned over egg and potato dishes. For lunch or dinner, it appears again with burritos, in enchiladas, or over grilled meats and roasted potatoes. This sauce is best when it is fresh or used within one day of being made.

1 Tbsp. CANOLA OIL
1/2 cup finely chopped ONION
2 GARLIC CLOVES, minced
2 Tbsp. ALL-PURPOSE or WHOLE-WHEAT FLOUR
1/4 tsp. GROUND CUMIN
SALT and PEPPER to taste
1 1/2 cups PORK or CHICKEN STOCK
1 cup chopped, roasted and peeled NEW MEXICO
    GREEN CHILES
1/4 tsp. DRIED OREGANO

In a medium saucepan over medium high heat, sauté the onion and garlic in the oil until tender, about 3 minutes. Stir in the flour, cumin, salt and pepper and cook over medium heat, stirring, for 2 minutes. Stir in the stock and simmer until thick and smooth. Stir in the chiles and oregano. At this point you may cover the pot and keep it in the refrigerator for up to one day. To serve, heat thoroughly.

Yields 2 cups.

Authentic New Mexico
Red Chile Sauce

Red chile sauce is preferred by many northern New Mexicans who have Hispanic roots and by most New Mexican old-timers. This may be partially explained by the fact that long ago, before freezers, only dried red chiles were available year-round. But, many natives actually prefer its distinctive taste. There's certainly no getting around red chile's coarse earthy flavors. It's for chile lovers only. Real New Mexicans would never think of diluting their red chile sauce with tomatoes. In enchilada dishes they may occasionally enrich it with a bit of cream, though. Red chile sauce can appear at any meal. It's also the essential ingredient for **Carne Adovada** *(see page 18).*

Today's cooks have discovered another advantage of red chile. It can be made in large batches ahead of time and kept frozen for up to 6 months until needed.

1 pound DRIED NEW MEXICO RED CHILE PODS, remove stems
(leave seeds and veins if you desire a hotter sauce)
2 heads of GARLIC, peeled
1 large ONION, chopped
2 Tbsp. DRIED OREGANO
1 tsp. SALT
WATER as necessary

Place the dried chile pods on a cookie sheet and place in a preheated 375 degree oven for just a few minutes until they become soft and leathery. Working in small batches at a time as will loosely fit into a blender or food processor, purée smooth the chile pods with the spices, adding small amounts of water as needed to make a sauce the consistency of thick cream. Place each batch of the puréed mixture in a large bowl until all the chiles have been blended. Stir the batches together to evenly disperse the seasonings.

Yields about 1 1/2 to 2 quarts.

Here's a special precaution when preparing red chiles. Cover all rubber or plastic parts of your blender with plastic wrap and use wooden or metal spoons. Otherwise, everything made of a porous material will be stained red permanently.

Green Chile Cilantro Pesto

This brilliant green pesto captures the flavor and heat of fresh green chiles. It is very rich so a little goes a long way. You can place it in one-half cup sized containers and freeze it for up to 6 months. That way, it will be instantly available to create fast and easy pastas and pizzas, to add to vegetable soups or rice to lend its succulent heat, and for topping grilled meats.

3 1/2 cups chopped, roasted and peeled NEW MEXICO
   GREEN CHILES
1 1/4 cups FRESH CILANTRO LEAVES (about 1 large bunch)
1 tsp. LIME ZEST
1 Tbsp. LIME JUICE
1 cup PINE NUTS
1/2 cup OLIVE OIL
4 GARLIC CLOVES, peeled
SALT to taste
1 cup grated PARMESAN or ROMANO CHEESE (or a blend
   of both)

In a blender or food processor add the chiles, cilantro, lime zest and juice, nuts, olive oil, garlic and salt. Purée until almost smooth. Stir in the grated cheese.

Yields about 5 cups.

Land of Enchantment Spice Mix

This vibrantly-flavored dry spice mix can be sprinkled on meats, vegetables or cheeses before cooking to lend an authentic New Mexican flavor. It will keep in an airtight container for about a year.

2 Tbsp. SALT
1 Tbsp. GREEN CHILE POWDER
2 tsp. NEW MEXICO RED CHILE POWDER
1 tsp. GROUND CUMIN
1 1/2 tsp. DRIED OREGANO
1/2 tsp. CHILE CARIBE
2 tsp. GRANULATED GARLIC
2 tsp. GRANULATED ONION

Toss all together.

Yields about 1/3 cup.

Sandstone Mayonnaise

This is no ordinary mayonnaise. It makes a wonderful bread spread for meat, cheese, vegetable or egg sandwiches. Use immediately or store in an airtight glass container in the refrigerator. It will keep well for up to 2 weeks.

1/4 cup MAYONNAISE (low fat may be used)
1 1/2 tsp. NEW MEXICO RED CHILE POWDER
1 tsp. WORCESTERSHIRE SAUCE
1 GARLIC CLOVE, crushed
1/4 tsp. GROUND CUMIN
1/2 tsp. SOY SAUCE
pinch CAYENNE

In a small bowl or jar, stir all of the ingredients together.

Yields about 1/3 cup.

Hot Cilantro Lime Oil

This flavored oil can be used to brush onto vegetables or meats while grilling and used in salad dressings. It may be stored, tightly covered, in the refrigerator for up to 6 hours.

Tips for cilantro: *Be sure to use the freshest cilantro leaves you can find because they rapidly lose their flavor with age. Even when stored tightly sealed in the refrigerator, they will only keep a day or two. Never substitute dried cilantro in any recipe because its grassy taste is nothing like fresh cilantro. If you can't find fresh cilantro in your area, this short-lived herb can be easily grown from seeds.*

1/4 cup LIME JUICE
1/3 cup plus 1 Tbsp. OLIVE OIL
2 Tbsp. LAND OF ENCHANTMENT SPICE MIX (see page 15)
1/4 cup chopped FRESH CILANTRO LEAVES

Whisk together.

Yields about 3/4 cup.

Chile Cumin Oil

This seasoned oil is wonderful for brushing on vegetables before grilling. Stored in an airtight glass jar in the refrigerator, it will keep for several weeks.

1/2 cup OLIVE OIL
1 1/2 tsp. NEW MEXICO RED CHILE POWDER
4 GARLIC CLOVES, crushed (or 1 tsp. GRANULATED GARLIC)
1 tsp. GROUND CUMIN
2 tsp. PREPARED MUSTARD
SALT and PEPPER to taste

In a small bowl or jar, combine all of the ingredients.

Yields about 1/2 cup.

Cactus Dressing

This flavorful green dressing is wonderful for pasta, greens and/or grilled meat salads. By using drained nonfat yogurt this dressing tastes rich and creamy without adding fat. Be sure to keep it tightly sealed in the refrigerator until you need it. Try to use it within a day or two while it's fresh.

3 Tbsp. chopped FRESH CILANTRO LEAVES
2 Tbsp. OLIVE OIL
1 tsp. LIME ZEST
1/4 cup LIME JUICE
2 tsp. GREEN CHILE POWDER (may substitute RED CHILE POWDER
     although you will lose the brilliant green color of
     this dressing)
1 tsp. PREPARED MUSTARD
3/4 tsp. GROUND CUMIN
2 GARLIC CLOVES, crushed
3 Tbsp. finely chopped, roasted and peeled NEW MEXICO
     GREEN CHILES
1/3 cup drained NONFAT PLAIN YOGURT* (or NONFAT SOUR
     CREAM)
1/4 tsp. each SALT and PEPPER

In a medium bowl, whisk all ingredients together.

Yields about 1 1/2 cups.

* Take 1 cup of nonfat plain yogurt and place it in a coffee filter lined funnel to drain into a bowl in the refrigerator for about 6 hours, until the yogurt is the consistency of sour cream. Discard the drained liquid.

New Mexico Sour Cream Dip

This tangy sour cream can be used to garnish any tortilla-based New Mexican dish, for dipping with meatballs and for serving with savory corn pancakes. It may be made ahead and kept, tightly covered, in the refrigerator for up to one day.

3 Tbsp. chopped, roasted and peeled NEW MEXICO GREEN CHILES
4 GARLIC CLOVES, crushed
1/4 cup chopped FRESH CILANTRO LEAVES
1/4 cup chopped GREEN ONIONS
1/4 tsp. TABASCO®
1/4 tsp. SALT
1/2 cup SOUR CREAM

Toss together and chill.

Yields about 1 1/4 cups.

Carne Adovada

Carne Adovada is served much like plain red chile sauce over egg, potato, bean and tortilla dishes. It is also the traditional filling for tamales.

3 cups prepared AUTHENTIC NEW MEXICO RED CHILE SAUCE, (see page 13)
1 pound PORK or BEEF STEW MEAT, cubed

Place the chile sauce and meat in a crock pot or heavy pot. Add about 1 1/2 cups water or beef stock, as needed. Cover and simmer gently until the meat is very tender. The completed sauce should be rich and thick, not watery. You can let it simmer all day in your crock pot, or in a covered pot for two to four hours.

Yields about 5 cups.

Chorizo

New Mexican **chorizo** *is decidedly different from the chorizo found in Mexican or Spanish markets. It is usually more flavorful, rich in spices and hot chiles, and is less fatty. This is a homemade version to use when this specialty of New Mexico's butchers is unavailable. Wrap it airtight in plastic and refrigerate for no more than one day. For longer storage, it may be frozen for up to 3 months.*

1 pound GROUND PORK
2 Tbsp. LIME JUICE
3 Tbsp. minced ONION
1/2 tsp. GROUND CUMIN
3 Tbsp. finely chopped, roasted and peeled NEW MEXICO
    GREEN CHILES
1 Tbsp. NEW MEXICO RED CHILE POWDER
1 tsp. DRIED OREGANO
2 tsp. PAPRIKA
1/2 tsp. SALT
1/4 tsp. CAYENNE

In a large bowl, mash all of the ingredients together. Form the mixture into rolls or patties. Fry it slowly in oil over medium heat until it is golden brown.

Yields about 1 pound.

APPETIZERS

Popeye's Green Dip

This hot chip dip tastes rich yet is lighter in fat than many cheese dips. It's also packed with vitamin-rich spinach.

1 tsp. CANOLA OIL
1/2 large ONION, minced
4 GARLIC CLOVES, crushed
1 TOMATO, seeded, chopped
1/4 cup chopped, roasted and peeled NEW MEXICO
    GREEN CHILES
1 bunch SPINACH LEAVES (8 oz.), chopped, steamed,
    squeezed dry
1/2 tsp. GROUND CUMIN
2 tsp. LEMON JUICE
6 ounces NEUFCHÂTEL or CREAM CHEESE
1 1/2 cups grated MOZZARELLA or JACK CHEESE
1/2 cup SKIM MILK
SALT and PEPPER to taste

In a saucepan, heat the oil over medium high heat and sauté the onion until softened, about 3 minutes. Add the garlic, tomato and chiles. Sauté one minute and remove from heat. Add the remaining ingredients and toss until combined. Butter a 1-quart baking dish and spoon the mixture into it. Top with 1/4 cup sliced olives and more cheese if desired. At this point, the dip may be covered and stored in the refrigerator for up to 8 hours.

To serve, preheat the oven to 450 degrees. Uncover the dish and bake at 450 degrees for 20-25 minutes until it's heated through. Serve with corn chips.

Yields 4 servings.

Christmas Eve Tamales

These traditional tamales can be found on the table of every New Mexican family on Christmas Eve. Because they are labor intensive, they are usually made in large batches and frozen for use throughout the year. They are enjoyed eaten out-of-hand as snacks or engulfed in red chile sauce and topped with cheese as a main dish.

Dough:
>   5 cups CORN MASA HARINA MIX
>   1/2 cup SHORTENING or LARD
>   3/4 tsp. SALT
>   3/4 tsp. BAKING POWDER
>   1 cup MEAT STOCK or water as needed

Filling:
>   1 quart CARNE ADOVADA (see page 18), meat shredded or
>   finely chopped

In a large bowl, beat the dough ingredients together with enough stock or water to make a soft fluffy dough. You may need to add additional water as the dough stands to keep it smooth. Soak 2 packages of dried corn husks in hot water until they've softened and pat them dry. Lay out one or more overlapping sheets of corn husks to form an 8 x 5 rectangle. Spoon about 3 tablespoons of the dough onto the corn husks and spread to a 1/4-inch thick rectangle in the center, about 3 x 2 inches in size. Spoon about 2 tablespoons of **Carne Adovada** onto the center and fold the longest sides towards the center until the dough meets and encloses the filling. Fold in the remaining sides and secure with narrow strips of corn husks. Repeat to make about 5 dozen tamales. At this point, completed tamales may be wrapped airtight and frozen for up to 1 year until needed.

To cook the tamales, place them, folded ends up, in a steamer over boiling water. You may use a colander set inside a large pot of water, making sure that the water does not touch the tamales. Steam, covered, for 1 to 1 1/2 hours until cooked. The dough will be firm and will have set.

Yields about 2 1/2 dozen tamales.

Hummingbird Bundles

These easy tortilla bundles will charm even the most sophisticated palates. The crisp buttery-crusted tortillas enclose the melting center. Inside, the Brie melds beautifully into the sweet spiciness of the mango salsa. Take care not to overbake these or the mango salsa will lose its vitality and sweetness.

3 cups FESTIVAL MANGO SALSA (see page 32)
8 ounces BRIE, sliced
6 FLOUR TORTILLAS
1 1/2 Tbsp. BUTTER, melted

Preheat your oven to 400 degrees. Divide the salsa and Brie slices among the flour tortillas and fold in all four sides to make a secure envelope bundle. Lightly oil a cookie sheet and place bundles on top. Brush bundles lightly with melted butter and bake at 400 degrees just until outsides are golden.

Yields 6 appetizer servings.

Cowboy Pinto Bean Dip

This cold bean dip is great for picnics as a sandwich spread or for dipping veggies or chips.

2 Tbsp. CANOLA OIL
1/2 cup finely chopped ONION
3 GARLIC CLOVES, minced
1 1/2 cups mashed cooked PINTO BEANS
1/4 cup SANDSTONE MAYONNAISE (see page 15)
1 tsp. DRIED OREGANO
2 Tbsp. minced FRESH CILANTRO LEAVES
1/2 cup grated CHEESE (any variety)
1/2 cup chopped NUTS
1 CARROT, finely grated

In a medium saucepan over medium high heat, sauté the onion and garlic in the oil until tender, about 3 minutes. Place in a bowl and toss in all of the remaining ingredients. Cover and chill.

Yields about 3 1/2 cups.

Trailblazer Bean Dip

This hot bean dip is simple to make. Serve it with corn chips and vegetables.

4 cups cooked ANASAZI BEANS, drained,
    reserving 2 Tbsp. cooking liquid (see page 82)
3 ounces CREAM CHEESE or NEUFCHÂTEL CHEESE
1/4 tsp. WORCESTERSHIRE SAUCE
2 tsp. NEW MEXICO RED CHILE POWDER
1 1/2 cups grated SHARP CHEDDAR CHEESE
4 GREEN ONIONS, chopped

Preheat the oven to 350 degrees. In a blender or food processor purée the beans, cream cheese, worcestershire and chile powder with cooking water as needed to form a smooth mixture. Grease a one-quart baking dish and spoon mixture into it. Toss the cheese and green onions together and sprinkle on top. At this point it may be covered and refrigerated for up to 8 hours.

To serve, preheat the oven to 350 degrees. Bake at 350 degrees until it is heated through and the top is golden, about 20 to 30 minutes.

Yields 6 servings.

Great Balls of Fire

These wonderful sausage chile balls are positively addictive. By keeping some handy in the freezer they will make easy last minute appetizers for impromptu gatherings. The **New Mexico Sour Cream Dip** *(on page 18) makes a great dipping sauce.*

1 1/2 cups WHOLE-WHEAT PASTRY or ALL-PURPOSE FLOUR
2 Tbsp. NON-INSTANT SKIM MILK POWDER, optional
2 tsp. BAKING POWDER
1/2 tsp. BAKING SODA
1/2 tsp. SALT
2 Tbsp. SHORTENING
8 ounces CHEDDAR CHEESE, grated
1 pound CHORIZO SAUSAGE, casings removed
1/2 cup chopped, roasted and peeled NEW MEXICO
    GREEN CHILES

In a large bowl, stir together the flour, milk powder, baking powder, soda, salt and shortening. With a fork or pastry cutter, cut the mixture until it is evenly crumbly. Using your hands, mix in the grated cheese, chorizo and chiles. Form the mixture into 1-inch balls. At this point, they may be wrapped tightly and frozen for up to 3 months until needed.

To serve, preheat the oven to 425 degrees. Lightly grease a cookie sheet and scatter the balls on top. Bake at 425 degrees for 15-20 minutes until golden brown. Serve hot.

Yields about 4 dozen.

Spiced Cherry Pecans

New Mexico cherries are highly valued treasures. When combined with local pecans and New Mexican spices they come alive. Store these prepared snacks in an airtight container, where they will keep for several days.

2 Tbsp. BUTTER, melted
1 Tbsp. NEW MEXICO RED CHILE POWDER
1/4 tsp. GROUND CUMIN
1/2 tsp. DRIED OREGANO
3/4 tsp. SALT
1/4 tsp. CAYENNE
1/2 tsp. GROUND CINNAMON
1 1/2 cups shelled PECAN HALVES
3/4 cup DRIED CHERRIES

Preheat the oven to 350 degrees. In a shallow baking dish (about 8-inches square or larger), toss the butter, seasonings, pecans and cherries. Bake at 350 degrees for 8 - 10 minutes, until the pecans are golden and fragrant. Place on paper towels until cool.

Yields about 2 1/2 cups.

Adobe Pink Spread

The spiciness of the pecans melded with the sweetness of the dried cherries becomes nirvana when blended with cream cheese. This lovely pink spread will keep several days in the refrigerator, tightly covered. Serve it cold with toasted bread, bagels or flour tortilla pieces.

2 cups SPICED CHERRY PECANS (see above), uniformly chopped
8 ounces CREAM CHEESE or NEUFCHÂTEL, softened

In a medium bowl, stir the chopped cherry pecans with the cream cheese until well combined.

Yields about 3 1/3 cups.

Weaver's Chile Rolls

Flour tortilla rolls, stuffed with savory chile fillings, are popular appetizers in New Mexico. This version, using spicy chile pesto is especially flavorful. Serve these within a few hours of making, being sure to keep them tightly covered in the refrigerator until needed.

1 cup GREEN CHILE CILANTRO PESTO (see page 14)
2 cups RICOTTA CHEESE
1 RED BELL PEPPER, roasted, peeled, seeded and chopped
3 GREEN ONIONS, minced
1/4 cup chopped pitted BLACK or GREEN OLIVES
8 large FLOUR TORTILLAS

In a medium bowl stir together the pesto, ricotta, bell pepper, green onions and olives. Divide the mixture among the flour tortillas, spreading evenly to cover the top of each. Roll them up and slice the rolls crosswise into 1 1/2-inch thick pieces.

Yields 4 - 8 servings.

Classic New Mexico Fondue

Most every New Mexican has a similar version of this popular hot cheese dip also known as chile con queso. Be sure to serve it with plenty of corn tortilla chips.

1 pound CHEDDAR CHEESE, grated
1/2 cup roasted, peeled and chopped NEW MEXICO GREEN CHILES
1 small TOMATO, seeded and chopped
2 Tbsp. minced ONION
1/4 tsp. WORCESTERSHIRE SAUCE
1/2 tsp. minced GARLIC
1/4 tsp. DRIED OREGANO
SALT and PEPPER to taste

In a large saucepan or fondue pot over low heat, slowly melt the cheese. Place the chiles, tomato and onion in a blender or food processor and pulse just to coarsely purée. Stir the purée into the melted cheese with the worcestershire, garlic, oregano, salt and pepper. Heat through, stirring, and serve hot.

Yields 4 - 6 servings.

Opera Empañadas with Goat Cheese & Jam

Empañadas are traditional little turnovers made of a leavened dough that is stuffed with sweet or savory fillings then baked or fried. They are especially loved during the Christmas holidays. Using wonton skins makes an updated turnover that assembles quickly with a minimum of fuss. After they are brushed with oil, they may be layered between wax paper and frozen for up to 3 months to be baked later.

24 WONTON SKINS
1/2 cup soft GOAT CHEESE
1/4 cup BIG JIM JAM (see page 101)

Place one teaspoonful of cheese on half of each wonton skin and top with 1/2 teaspoonful of jam. Moisten the edges of the won tons and fold over, pinching to seal edges.

Preheat the oven to 400 degrees. Oil a baking sheet with canola oil. Brush the wontons lightly with canola oil and place on the baking sheet. Bake at 400 degrees for 10-15 minutes until lightly golden. Sprinkle very lightly with salt or sugar and serve.

Yields 24 wonton empañadas.

Volcanic Nachos

Nachos are popular snacking fare throughout New Mexico. They are usually made by piling refried beans, cheese, sour cream and guacamole onto corn tortilla chips. Although nachos are messy finger foods, locals enjoy them with beer or frosty margaritas. These more sophisticated versions are slightly lighter yet even more flavorful than the usual renditions.

4 FLOUR TORTILLAS
2 heads of GARLIC, roasted*, peeled, chopped
2 medium AVOCADOS, peeled, pitted, diced
1/2 cup chopped GREEN ONIONS
3/4 cup chopped, roasted and peeled NEW MEXICO
   GREEN CHILES
3 ROMA TOMATOES, seeded, diced
1/2 cup sliced GREEN OLIVES (optional)
1/2 cup chopped FRESH CILANTRO LEAVES
1 1/2 cups grated CHEESE

Preheat the oven to 400 degrees. Place the tortillas on cookie sheets and sprinkle with remaining ingredients. Bake at 400 degrees until the cheese has melted, about 10 minutes. Cut into snack-sized pieces.

Yields 4 - 8 servings.

* To roast garlic: trim the tops of the garlic heads to expose the cloves, drizzle with 1 tsp. olive oil and sprinkle with ground black pepper. Seal in foil or place in a garlic roaster and bake at 325 degrees for about 45 minutes until tender. Once cool, squeeze the cloves from the base to remove the flesh from the peels.

Guacamole

Originating in Mexico over 2,000 years ago, avocados are named for the Aztec word "Ahuacatl". Although avocados didn't make their way into New Mexico until the 1940's, they have become a vital part of our cuisine. Guacamole is the most popular way to enjoy avocados and every New Mexican has their own version of it. Use it to top nachos, tortilla dishes, eggs or simply as a cold dip for chips. Once made, keep guacamole tightly covered in the refrigerator and serve as soon as possible because it darkens with age or exposure to air.

3 AVOCADOS, peeled, seeded and mashed
3 Tbsp. LIME JUICE
3 GARLIC CLOVES, crushed
1/4 cup minced ONIONS
1/4 cup chopped, roasted and peeled NEW MEXICO
 GREEN CHILES
SALT, PEPPER, TABASCO®, and WORCESTERSHIRE SAUCE to taste
1 small TOMATO, seeded, chopped

Place all of the ingredients in a medium bowl and mash using a fork to a coarse purée.

Yields about 2 1/2 cups.

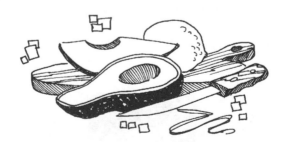

SALSAS

A Word about Salsa

Salsa means "sauce" in Spanish. Throughout New Mexico it has come to mean any cold sauce using chiles. Salsas have expanded beyond traditional recipes to contain any variety of vegetables, fruits and herbs with chiles. As powerhouses of fresh flavors and textures, they make perfect lowfat condiments. They are used on virtually everything to add zip, much like many people will use ketchup. Salsas made at home using fresh ingredients are always best served as soon as possible. Most will keep, tightly covered, in the refrigerator for a few hours or even a day. But, never freeze a salsa. It won't recover.

Taos Salsa

Every northern New Mexico family has their own version of this traditional salsa. What sets these salsas apart from modern versions is the use of a pinch of cinnamon or allspice. This adds a distinctive, yet illusive, flavor while bringing out the natural sweetness of the tomatoes. To make this simple salsa, you absolutely must have homegrown, vine-ripened tomatoes for their fresh tomato flavor.

2 large fresh TOMATOES, peeled
3/4 cup chopped, roasted and peeled NEW MEXICO
**   GREEN CHILES**
3 GARLIC CLOVES
1/2 cup chopped ONION
2 Tbsp. VINEGAR
2 tsp. CHILE CARIBE
1 tsp. GROUND CINNAMON
SALT to taste

Place all of the ingredients in a blender or food processor and pulse until coarsely puréed. This salsa will keep in the refrigerator longer than most, up to 3 days.

Yields 2 1/2 cups.

Piñata Fruit Salsa

I love the colorful combination of tropical fruits in this light salsa. It makes a wonderful accompaniment to grilled seafood or chicken and a great topping for cheese tostadas. This salsa is best when served the same day it is made.

8 ounce can PINEAPPLE SLICES, drained, diced
1 MANGO, peeled, pitted, diced
1 1/2 cups sliced, FRESH STRAWBERRIES
1/2 large RED BELL PEPPER, seeded, diced
1/4 cup chopped, roasted and peeled NEW MEXICO
    GREEN CHILES
3 GREEN ONIONS, chopped
1/4 cup chopped FRESH CILANTRO LEAVES
1 Tbsp. grated GINGERROOT
3 Tbsp. LIME JUICE
1 Tbsp. OLIVE OIL

In a large bowl, toss all of the ingredients together.

Yields about 5 cups.

Rainbow Salsa

This sweet and savory salsa adds a splash of color to any dish. It is best when served cold soon after it is made.

1 ripe TOMATO, seeded, diced
1 MANGO, peeled, pitted, diced
1 large AVOCADO, peeled, pitted, diced
1/2 RED BELL PEPPER, seeded, diced (about 1/3 cup)
1/4 cup chopped GREEN ONIONS
3 Tbsp. chopped FRESH CILANTRO LEAVES
3 Tbsp. LIME JUICE
3 Tbsp. chopped, roasted and peeled NEW MEXICO
    GREEN CHILES
1/4 tsp. SALT
2 Tbsp. OLIVE OIL
1 1/2 Tbsp. ORANGE LIQUEUR

In a large bowl, toss all ingredients together.

Yields about 5 cups.

Conquistador Green Olive Salsa

Spanish olives come together with New Mexico chiles in this splendid, tart green salsa. It is the perfect accompaniment to grilled meats, pasta and green salads. Unlike many salsas, this one can be refrigerated tightly covered for up to one week.

1 1/2 cups SPANISH GREEN OLIVE PIECES
2 Tbsp. OLIVE OIL
3 large GARLIC CLOVES, crushed
3 Tbsp. chopped, roasted and peeled NEW MEXICO GREEN CHILES
1/2 cup chopped FRESH CILANTRO LEAVES
1 tsp. LEMON ZEST
2 Tbsp. LEMON JUICE
1 tsp. SPICY PREPARED MUSTARD

In a blender or food processor, pulse the olives and olive oil until coarsely chopped. Place in a bowl and add remaining ingredients. Add ground black pepper to taste. Although the olives are salty, it may need just a pinch of salt to taste.

Yields about 1 1/4 cup.

Festival Mango Salsa

Mangos are prolific in New Mexico markets because our neighbors south of the border grow plenty of them. The sweetness of ripe mangos perfectly complements the hotness of chiles. This is one of my favorite salsas. It can be stored, tightly covered, in the refrigerator for up to one day.

3 MANGOS, peeled, pitted and diced
1 cup chopped FRESH CILANTRO LEAVES (about one large bunch)
5 large GREEN ONIONS, chopped
1/4 cup chopped, roasted and peeled NEW MEXICO
**   GREEN CHILES**
3 Tbsp. LIME JUICE
3 GARLIC CLOVES, crushed
3 Tbsp. OLIVE OIL
1/4 tsp. SALT or to taste

In a medium bowl, toss all the ingredients together. Serve chilled.

Yields about 4 cups.

TORTILLA DISHES

Fluffy Flour Tortillas

2 cups WHOLE-WHEAT PASTRY or ALL-PURPOSE FLOUR
1/4 cup NON-INSTANT SKIM MILK POWDER
2 tsp. BAKING POWDER
3/4 tsp. SALT
2 Tbsp. SHORTENING

In a large bowl, stir together the flour, milk powder, baking powder and salt. With a fork or pastry cutter, mix in the shortening until it resembles coarse crumbs. Add just enough water to make a soft dough, about 1/2 cup, and knead it for 5 minutes on a lightly floured surface. Cover the dough with a damp towel and let it rest for about 30 minutes. Form the dough into 5 balls of equal size. Roll each ball out to a 1/8-inch thick circle, keeping the edges slightly thicker than the center by not rolling all the way to the edges. Keep the rolled out tortillas covered with the damp towel to prevent them from drying out. Heat a well-seasoned, but ungreased, iron skillet over medium-high heat. Place a tortilla in the skillet while gently shaking the skillet. It should slip around on the bottom of the skillet as it gently bubbles up and lightly browns on the bottom in a spotty pattern. If your skillet is the correct temperature, this will take only half a minute. Flip the tortilla over like a pancake and lightly brown the second side. Keep the freshly-made tortilla warm on a covered plate while you make the rest. Most New Mexicans use special clay tortilla warmers to hold their tortillas before serving. If you don't have one, you can use two glass pie plates as warmers by inverting the second one over the bottom plate.

This recipe yields 5 large tortillas.

ENCHILADAS

Enchiladas are probably the oldest of the New Mexican dishes featuring corn tortillas. They are made by layering corn tortillas with fillings, chile sauce and cheese and then baking. Real New Mexicans never roll their tortillas when making enchiladas, but merely stack the ingredients. Historically, the tortillas were first softened by dipping them in hot fat before incorporating them into the dish. Nowadays, you can achieve the same (and more heart-healthy) results by dipping them into chile sauce. Enchiladas should be baked as soon as they are assembled because they become soggy when allowed to sit for any length of time.

Plain Red Chile Enchiladas

In the oldest New Mexican cookbooks you'll find recipes for basic red chile enchiladas like these. They remain as popular today as they were a hundred years ago. Traditionally, these are topped simply with a fried egg. You'll find modern New Mexican cooks embellishing this recipe with additional meat, vegetable, cheese and nut fillings.

3 cups AUTHENTIC NEW MEXICO RED CHILE SAUCE (see page 13)
12 CORN TORTILLAS
3/4 cup finely chopped ONION
2 1/2 cups grated MILD WHITE or GOAT CHEESE

Oil an 8 or 9-inch square baking dish. Preheat the oven to 350 degrees. Dip the tortillas into the red chile sauce and place 4 on the bottom of the dish. Sprinkle with 1/4 cup of the onions and a third of the cheese. Repeat two more times, making three layers. Bake at 350 degrees for about 30 minutes until hot throughout and the cheese is golden.

Yields 4 servings.

Geronimo Chorizo Enchiladas

Hardier versions of enchiladas, such as these chorizo enchiladas, are favorites among real New Mexicans. Packed with red and green chiles, there's no ignoring their fiery potential.

12 CORN TORTILLAS
1 pound CHORIZO diced or crumbled
1 ONION, chopped
1/2 cup chopped, roasted and peeled NEW MEXICO
     GREEN CHILES
2 cups AUTHENTIC NEW MEXICO RED CHILE SAUCE (see page 13)
SALT to taste
2 1/2 cups grated CHEESE of choice

Place tortillas on a lightly oiled cookie sheet and bake at 375 degrees until hot and fragrant, about 5 minutes. Reserve. In a large heavy skillet over medium high heat fry the chorizo until it's no longer pink. Add the onion and continue to fry until the onion is soft and the chorizo golden, about 5 minutes. Stir in the green chiles, red chile sauce and salt to taste. Remove from heat. Oil an 8 or 9-inch baking dish and preheat the oven to 350 degrees. Place 4 tortillas on the bottom of the dish, top with a third of the sauce and a third of the cheese. Repeat two more times, making three layers. Bake at 350 degrees for about 35 minutes, until hot, bubbly and the top is golden.   Garnish with lettuce, tomato, cilantro and avocado as desired.

Yields 4 servings.

Enchanted Green Enchiladas

*Historically, green chile enchiladas can be as simple as the **Plain Red Chile Enchiladas** recipe on page 37, but are more often enriched with sour cream or heavy cream and eggs. This version substitutes skim milk thickened with skim milk powder for the heavy cream. By briefly baking the tortillas instead of dipping them in oil to soften, they become pliable and fragrant without the added fat. You won't notice the loss of calories.*

12 CORN TORTILLAS

The Sauce:
- **3/4 cup SKIM MILK**
- **2 Tbsp. NON-INSTANT SKIM MILK POWDER**
- **1 EGG, beaten**
- **1 cup chopped, roasted and peeled NEW MEXICO GREEN CHILES**
- **2 large TOMATOES, chopped or partially puréed**
- **SALT and PEPPER to taste**

Layer With:
- **1/2 ONION, chopped**
- **2 1/2 cups grated CHEDDAR or any MILD WHITE CHEESE**

Place tortillas on a lightly oiled cookie sheet and bake at 375 degrees until hot and fragrant, about 5 minutes. Reserve.

In a blender, place the milk, milk powder and egg and purée until smooth. Add the chiles and tomato and pulse just to combine. Season to taste. (If you prefer, you may substitute light cream for the milk and milk powder.)

Oil a 9-inch glass baking dish and preheat the oven to 375 degrees. Place 4 tortillas on the bottom of the dish, top with a third of the onions, a third of the cheese and a third of the sauce. Repeat two more times, making three layers. Bake at 375 degrees for about 35 minutes, until hot, bubbly and the top is golden.

Yields 4 servings.

Chicken Enchilada Indulgence

Most chicken enchiladas made by New Mexicans have a decidedly "south of the border" influence. This recipe is packed with all of the ingredients that make chicken enchiladas so popular.

12 CORN TORTILLAS
1 pound boneless skinless CHICKEN BREASTS, diced
4 GARLIC CLOVES, minced
1 1/2 tsp. CHILE CARIBE
12 ounces BEER
3 ounces CREAM CHEESE
2 cups CREAM or EVAPORATED SKIM MILK, divided
1 1/2 cups SLICED BLACK OLIVES
1 cup chopped, roasted and peeled NEW MEXICO GREEN CHILES
8 ounces grated SHARP CHEDDAR CHEESE, divided
6 large GREEN ONIONS, chopped
10 ounces GREEN TOMATILLAS
3 SERRANO CHILES, seeded, chopped
1/4 cup chopped FRESH CILANTRO LEAVES
1 tsp. GROUND CUMIN
SALT and PEPPER to taste
1 EGG

Place tortillas on a lightly oiled cookie sheet and bake at 375 degrees until fragrant, about 5 minutes. Reserve. In a medium bowl, stir together the diced chicken, garlic, caribe and beer. Cover and let marinate in the refrigerator for 1 to 8 hours. Place the mixture in a large saucepan over medium high heat and simmer until the chicken is no longer pink, about 5 - 8 minutes. Remove the chicken to a medium bowl and reserve separately 1/4 cup of the cooking liquid, discarding the rest. Add the cream cheese, 1/2 cup of the cream, olives, green chiles, 4 ounces of the cheddar and the green onions. Stir to combine. In a blender or food processor place the tomatillas, serrano chiles, cilantro, cumin, salt, pepper, egg, reserved beer cooking liquid and 1 1/2 cups of the cream. Blend to a coarse purée. Oil a 9 or 10 -inch baking dish and preheat the oven to 350 degrees. Layer 4 tortillas on the bottom of the prepared dish, top with a third of the chicken mixture then a third of the blender mixture. Repeat two more times, making three layers. Sprinkle the last 4 ounces of cheddar on top. Bake at 350 degrees until hot, about 35 minutes.

Yields 4 - 6 servings.

BURRITOS

Burritos are flour tortillas that have been wrapped around a hot filling. Traditionally, tortillas are filled down the center simply with refried beans, cheese and chiles. The tortillas are then rolled around the filling, with the bottom end folded inside to hold in the filling. Popular throughout the southwest, New Mexicans have made burritos their own. They are our fast food and are frequently eaten out-of-hand just as other Americans eat hamburgers. Stuffed with everything imaginable nowadays, they are a meal in themselves. Burritos can also be made into a more "sit-down" dish by smothering them with chile sauce, topping with cheese, and serving them on a plate.

Green Mesa Burritos

This is one of the finest recipes for guacamole lovers! Be careful not to overbake these or the guacamole will darken and become bitter.

2 1/2 cups GUACAMOLE (see page 30)
4 - 6 FLOUR TORTILLAS
2 cups TRADITIONAL-STYLE NEW MEXICO GREEN CHILE
   SAUCE (see page 12)
1 1/4 cups grated CHEESE of choice

Oil a 9-inch baking dish and preheat the oven to 350 degrees. Place about 1/2 cup of **Guacamole** down the middle of each flour tortilla and roll each one. Place the rolls in the baking dish in a single layer with the seam sides down. Pour the **Green Chile Sauce** on top and sprinkle with the cheese. Bake at 350 degrees just until the cheese is melted and golden, about 10 minutes.

Yields 4 servings.

Ballooning Breakfast Burritos

Albuquerque, New Mexico is the ballooning capital of the world and hosts the International Balloon Fiesta each October. Giant breakfast burritos are traditional fare for spectators. They are especially warming on chilly mornings.

8 ounces CHORIZO or any other meat desired, chopped
1 medium POTATO (8 ounces), diced, boiled tender
4 EGGS, beaten with 1 tsp. MILK
4 FLUFFY FLOUR TORTILLAS, warmed (see page 36)
1 cup cooked ANASAZI BEANS (see page 82), drained
3/4 - 1 cup grated CHEESE of choice
3/4 cup chopped, roasted and peeled NEW MEXICO GREEN CHILES, or 2 cups heated TRADITIONAL-STYLE NEW MEXICO GREEN CHILE SAUCE (see page12)

In a large heavy skillet, fry the chorizo over medium high heat until browned. Remove the meat to a paper towel to drain. Add the potatoes to the skillet and fry until golden brown. Season with salt and pepper and remove to a bowl. Add a teaspoon of oil to the skillet if needed and lower the heat to medium. Pour in the beaten eggs and cook until set.

To make burritos for eating out-of-hand, place one quarter of the potatoes, chorizo, eggs, beans, cheese and chopped green chiles down the center of each flour tortilla. Roll up and fold over the bottom end to hold in the filling. Eat while hot or wrap tightly in foil and reheat in the oven when ready to serve.

To make burritos for serving on a plate, preheat the oven to 350 degrees. Assemble the burritos as above, omitting the chopped green chiles and using only half of the cheese. Oil a 9-inch baking dish and line the burritos seam side down in the dish. Pour the **Green Chile Sauce** (or the chopped chiles) over the burritos and sprinkle with the rest of the cheese. Bake at 350 degrees just to heat through and melt the cheese, about 10 minutes.

Yields 4 servings.

Carne Adovada Burritos

These are popular burritos for any meal of the day.

1 Tbsp. CANOLA OIL
1 medium POTATO (8 ounces), diced, boiled tender
SALT and PEPPER to taste
4 EGGS, beaten with 1 tsp. MILK
4 FLUFFY FLOUR TORTILLAS, warmed (see page 36)
2 cups CARNE ADOVADA (see page 18), meat chopped
3/4 - 1 cup grated MILD WHITE CHEESE (part GOAT CHEESE makes
**   a nice complement to the chile sauce)**
2 cups heated AUTHENTIC NEW MEXICO RED CHILE SAUCE
**   (see page 13)**

In a large heavy skillet over medium high heat fry the potatoes until golden brown. Season with salt and pepper and remove to a bowl. Add another tsp. of oil to the skillet if needed and lower the heat to medium. Pour in the beaten eggs and cook until set.

To make burritos for eating out-of-hand place one quarter of the potatoes, *Carne Adovada*, eggs and cheese down the center of each flour tortilla. Roll up and fold over bottom end to hold in filling. Eat while hot or wrap tightly in foil and reheat in the oven when ready to serve.

To make burritos for serving on a plate, preheat the oven to 350 degrees. Assemble the burritos as above, using only half of the cheese. Oil a 9-inch baking dish and line the burritos seam side down in the dish. Pour the *Red Chile Sauce* over the burritos and sprinkle with the rest of the cheese. Bake at 350 degrees just to heat through and melt the cheese, about 10 minutes.

Yields 4 servings.

Route 66 Nachos

Sure, nachos are usually served as appetizers, but plenty of natives will also make a meal of them. This version, healthier than the usual sour cream and guacamole-laden versions, eats out-of-hand with less mess. By mashing spicy cooked beans instead of frying them in oil, these offer a less fattening version of "refried beans" that are just as rich in flavor. Also, in this recipe the corn tortillas are crisped by being baked with the toppings, instead of fried in oil as in traditional recipes. For the ultimate in a low fat nacho, use a low fat cheese. This basic recipe can become a more gourmet indulgence by using fancier cheeses and any good homemade chunky salsa.

8 CORN TORTILLAS
**2 cups mashed cooked ANASAZI BEANS (see page 82), or
      a 16 ounce can of REFRIED BEANS**
1 1/2 cups crumbled soft GOAT CHEESE (or any mild cheese)
1 cup of prepared SALSA of choice

Preheat oven to 350 degrees. Place the corn tortillas on cookie sheets and spread each with about 1/4 cup of the mashed beans. Sprinkle about 3 tablespoons of cheese on top of each. Bake at 350 degrees until they are hot and the cheese is golden, about 10-15 minutes. Place them on serving plates and top each with 2 table-spoons of salsa.

Yields 8 nachos.

Sheepherder's Nachos

These original nachos combine some of the finest native New Mexico ingredients into a main dish tortilla "pizza."

2 tsp. CANOLA OIL
3 cups lean LAMB MEAT, julienned
3 TOMATOES, finely chopped
1 tsp. GROUND CUMIN
1 tsp. DRIED OREGANO
2 GARLIC CLOVES, crushed
2 tsp. NEW MEXICO RED CHILE POWDER
1/4 cup smooth or chunky PEANUT BUTTER
4 - 6 FLOUR TORTILLAS
3 cups torn LETTUCE LEAVES
2/3 cup chopped, roasted and peeled NEW MEXICO
    GREEN CHILES
1/2 cup minced RED ONION
6-8 ounces soft GOAT CHEESE (or any mild cheese), crumbled

In a large skillet, fry the lamb in the oil over medium high heat for 3 minutes, stirring. Add the tomatoes and spices and continue to fry until the meat is no longer pink, about 5 minutes. Stir in the peanut butter, with enough water to make a smooth sauce. Place the flour tortillas on ovenproof serving plates and top with the lettuce. Divide the meat mixture among the tortillas and top with the chiles, onion and goat cheese. You may serve them immediately or place them under the broiler for a few minutes to soften the cheese.

Yields 4 servings.

Corazon Tostadas

Tostadas have come to mean any tortilla that is stacked high with flavorful toppings. Traditionally, the tortillas are fried, but this isn't really necessary because they are completely buried anyway. I think this less greasy version allows the freshness of all the ingredients to meld more pleasingly. These are certainly more heart-healthy which is why they've been named "corazon," the Spanish word for heart. You'll love them.

3/4 pound CHICKEN MEAT, julienned
2 tsp. LAND OF ENCHANTMENT SPICE MIX (see page 15)
1 1/2 tsp. CANOLA OIL
6 large FLOUR TORTILLAS
2 cups of ANASAZI BEANS (see page 82), drained, partially
    mashed if desired, kept hot
4-6 ounces GOAT CHEESE, crumbled
2 cups LETTUCE LEAVES, torn
4 - 5 cups RAINBOW SALSA (see page 33)

Toss the chicken with the spice mix. Heat the oil in a small skillet over medium high heat and fry the chicken pieces until they are golden and tender. Place the tortillas on serving plates. Top with the beans, goat cheese, lettuce, salsa and chicken.

Yields 4 - 6 servings.

THE CHILE SOUP POT

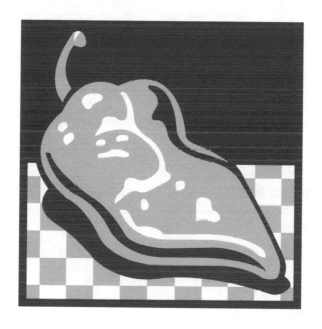

Simple yet hardy soups are welcome suppers for most New Mexicans. Evenings are cool here, the result of our high altitudes and dry air. Steaming bowls of chile are also in keeping with our more relaxed styles of eating. These are always served with fresh flour tortillas or bread.

History Book Green Chile Stew

Green chile stew recipes are carefully guarded secrets among New Mexican families. Everyone has their favorite version of this popular stew. This is my best green chile stew recipe. It is rich in flavor and makes a nourishing main dish.

8 ounces lean PORK, diced
1 Tbsp. FLOUR
1 Tbsp. CANOLA or OLIVE OIL
1 large BAKING POTATO (about 12 ounces), diced
1 1/2 cups chopped TOMATOES
1/2 cup chopped, roasted and peeled NEW MEXICO
**   GREEN CHILES**
2 GARLIC CLOVES, minced
1/2 tsp. NEW MEXICO RED CHILE POWDER
1 quart CHICKEN STOCK
1/2 tsp. GROUND CUMIN

Sprinkle the pork with flour to lightly coat. In a large saucepan, heat the oil over high heat and fry the meat until it's golden. Add the remaining ingredients and lower the heat to medium low. Cover the pan and simmer until the meat is very tender, about 4 hours. Alternately, you may cook the stew in a covered crock pot for 6 to 8 hours. Serve with flour tortillas.

Yields 4 serving.

Christmas Eve Posole

Posole is lime-treated corn kernels, called "hominy" in other areas of the country. Although it is sometimes found frozen, most New Mexicans use the more readily available dried versions. Dried posole has the added advantage of being more flavorful because as it cooks it will absorb the spicy cooking liquid. In fact, towards the end of their cooking time, posole will "pop" and become fluffy flowers with a rich corn taste and soft chewy texture. Real New Mexicans would never substitute water-logged canned hominy in their posole recipes.

In New Mexico the term posole also refers to the stew made out of posole corn. Posole made with red chiles is the mandatory dish for Christmas Eve celebrations. This is my spicy version of this popular holiday stew.

2 cups DRIED POSOLE CORN
1/2 - 1 pound BEEF or PORK STEW MEAT
2 cups AUTHENTIC NEW MEXICO RED CHILE SAUCE (see page 13)
BEEF STOCK as necessary to cover the posole by 1 1/2 inches
with liquid

Place all of the ingredients into a crock pot, cover and simmer for 8-12 hours until the posole is puffed and tender. Add additional stock or water if necessary as the posole absorbs the stock during the last few hours of cooking time. Posole must not be watery but should have just enough juices to require a spoon to eat. Salt to taste and serve with flour tortillas.

Yields 4 - 6 servings.

Indian Market Chile

This fresh tasting soup has virtually no fat, making it as popular for today's health-minded New Mexicans as it was for the ancient Indians of our past.

3/4 pound boneless skinless CHICKEN BREAST (one whole breast), chopped
4 cups CHICKEN STOCK
2/3 cup chopped ONION
1 GARLIC CLOVE, crushed
1 each ZUCCHINI and SUMMER SQUASH, chopped
2 TOMATOES, seeded, chopped
1 1/2 cups CORN KERNELS (fresh or frozen)
1/2 cup chopped, roasted and peeled NEW MEXICO GREEN CHILES
3 Tbsp. chopped FRESH CILANTRO LEAVES
1 tsp. GROUND CUMIN
1 tsp. DRIED OREGANO
SALT and PEPPER to taste

Place all ingredients in a large pot and stir. Simmer one or more hours over medium-low heat, covered, until all are tender.

Yields 4 servings.

Territorial Chile Posole Stew

By combining the best of green chile stew with the hardiness of posole, this stew is the ultimate New Mexico treat. It is my best stew for cold winter nights.

1 1/2 Tbsp. CANOLA OIL
3/4 pound PORK or BEEF STEW MEAT, cubed
SALT and PEPPER to taste
1 medium ONION, chopped
4 GARLIC CLOVES, minced
6 cups rich CHICKEN, BEEF or VEGETABLE STOCK
2 cups DRIED POSOLE CORN (see intro on page 49)
3/4 cup chopped, roasted and peeled NEW MEXICO
    GREEN CHILES
1 tsp. DRIED OREGANO
1/4 cup chopped FRESH CILANTRO LEAVES
1 medium POTATO (8 ounces), diced
3/4 pound CHORIZO, diced and browned

In a large skillet, heat the oil over medium high heat. Season the meat to taste with salt and pepper. Add the meat to the skillet and fry, tossing, until it is lightly golden brown. Lower the heat to medium and add the onion and garlic. Sauté until the onion is tender, about 5 minutes. Place the skillet mixture into a crock pot and add the rest of the ingredients. Cover, and let it simmer all day (about 8 - 12 hours depending on the heat of your crock pot), until the posole has popped and is tender. During the last few hours you may need to add additional stock or water if your posole is absorbing lots of liquid, making the stew too dry. Salt the stew to taste. Sprinkle with additional cilantro, if desired, and serve.

Yields 6 - 8 servings.

Chorizo Soup

Here is the ultimate comfort food. I've taken a creamy polenta-like soup and richly seasoned it with New Mexico ingredients, then given it one last bit of indulgence by adding a dollop of spicy pesto. This soup goes together effortlessly, making it perfect for any meal.

8 ounces CHORIZO, casings removed
1/2 cup chopped ONION
4 GARLIC CLOVES, minced
1/2 cup chopped, roasted and peeled NEW MEXICO
GREEN CHILES
3 cups BEAN or CHICKEN STOCK
1/2 cup CORNMEAL
1/2 cup grated MILD CHEESE
2 Tbsp. GREEN CHILE CILANTRO PESTO (see page 14)

In a large heavyweight saucepan over medium high heat fry the chorizo until it is golden. Crumble. Drain off any excess fat and add the onion and garlic. Lower the heat and sauté until the onions are softened, about 5 minutes. Stir in the stock and cornmeal. Bring to a gentle simmer and cook, stirring frequently, until creamy, about 35 minutes. Place the cheese and pesto on top and swirl them gently into the soup.

Yields 4 servings.

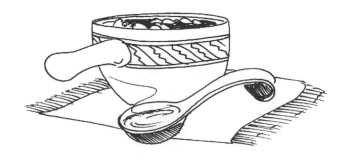

Pueblo Corn Jerky Stew

The use of dried corn has its roots in the cooking of the Pueblo Indians of our state. When cooked, dried corn retains a pleasing chewiness and rich corn flavor. Although only one ounce of dried beef jerky is used in this recipe, it supplies just the right amount of its distinctive rich beefy taste. This soup's creaminess comes from skim milk thickened with milk powder, instead of fat-laden cream.

2 cups DRIED CORN, soaked overnight, drained
3 cups BEEF STOCK
1/2 cup chopped, roasted and peeled NEW MEXICO
     GREEN CHILES
1 1/2 tsp. NEW MEXICO RED CHILE POWDER
1 Tbsp. MAPLE SYRUP
3 Tbsp. shredded BEEF JERKY (1 ounce)
3 GARLIC CLOVES, crushed
1 cup SKIM MILK
2 Tbsp. NON-INSTANT SKIM MILK POWDER
1 Tbsp. ALL-PURPOSE FLOUR

Place the corn, stock, chile, chile powder, syrup, jerky and garlic in a crock pot. Cover and simmer all day (8 - 10 hours) until the corn is tender. Blend the milk, powder and flour together until smooth and stir into the soup. Heat through until the soup has thickened. Season to taste with salt and pepper.

Yields 4 servings.

Aztec Blanco Chile

A bowl of this creamy stew, piled high with toppings, makes a simple and homey main dish.

1 1/2 Tbsp. CANOLA OIL
1 cup chopped ONION
4 GARLIC CLOVES, peeled, minced
1 1/2 cups chopped, roasted and peeled NEW MEXICO
    GREEN CHILES
2 tsp. CUMIN SEEDS, lightly crushed
3/4 cup dry roasted, unsalted PEANUTS
1/4 cup grated PARMESAN or ROMANO CHEESE
1 1/2 cups diced CHICKEN or TURKEY
3/4 cup EVAPORATED MILK
SALT and PEPPER to taste
1 pound RED POTATOES, boiled tender, quartered (about
    3 medium potatoes)
3 boiled EGGS, quartered
12 ripe BLACK OLIVES

In a large heavy saucepan heat the oil over medium high heat. Add the onions and garlic and sauté until the onions are tender, about 3 minutes. Add the chiles, cumin, peanuts, parmesan and meat. Heat through, stirring often. Stir in the milk, salt and pepper. Place in 3 serving bowls and top each with one third of the potatoes, eggs and olives.

Yields 3 servings.

Chilled Chamisa Soup

This cold soup, with a soft green color reminiscent of the native chamisa plants which blanket New Mexico deserts, is creamy and refreshing. Serve it as an elegant first course or to accompany a simple soup-and-sandwich luncheon. It can be made in minutes and kept in the refrigerator for several hours until you're ready to serve it.

1 cup rich CHICKEN STOCK
1/2 cup finely chopped RED ONION
2 medium AVOCADOS, peeled and seeded
1 Tbsp. LIME JUICE
1 Tbsp. chopped FRESH CILANTRO LEAVES
1/4 tsp. GREEN CHILE POWDER
pinch CAYENNE
1/4 tsp. SALT or to taste
1 cup NONFAT PLAIN YOGURT

In a blender, purée all of the ingredients until they are smooth. Place the purée in a tightly covered bowl and refrigerate for 4 hours until it's cold. Sprinkle with extra chopped cilantro and diced tomatoes for garnish when serving.

Yields 2 servings of about 1 1/2 cups each.

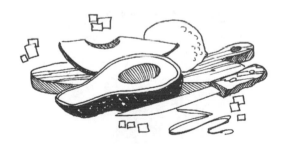

Feast Day Pumpkin Stew

Pumpkin, chiles and corn are foods native to New Mexico and frequently found in traditional Indian stews. This updated version is invigorated with chorizo and given a pleasing creaminess by the addition of milk.

1 tsp. CANOLA OIL
3/4 cup finely chopped ONION (about 1 medium)
3 GARLIC CLOVES, mashed
8 ounces CHORIZO, chopped
4 cups diced PUMPKIN PULP (or POTATOES)
1 1/2 cups rich CHICKEN or VEGETABLE STOCK
2 cups SKIM MILK
1/2 cup chopped, roasted and peeled NEW MEXICO
    GREEN CHILES
1/2 tsp. GROUND CUMIN
SALT to taste
1 1/2 cups DRIED CORN KERNELS or cooked POSOLE CORN

In a large heavy saucepan, heat the oil over medium high heat. Add the onion and garlic and sauté until they've softened, about 3 minutes. Add the chorizo and sauté until no longer pink, about 5 minutes. Add the pumpkin (or potatoes), stock, milk, chiles, cumin and salt. Simmer, partially covered, over medium-low heat until the pumpkin is tender. Add the corn and heat through. Serve it in bowls, sprinkled with any cheese desired for garnish.

Yields 4 servings.

MAIN DISHES

Huevos Benedict

"Huevos" is the Spanish word for eggs. This New Mexico version of Eggs Benedict is rich in regional flavors.

Biscuits:
  1 1/4 cups WHOLE-WHEAT PASTRY or ALL-PURPOSE FLOUR
  1/2 cup CORNMEAL
  3/4 tsp. BAKING SODA
  3/4 tsp. BAKING POWDER
  1/4 tsp. SALT
  5 Tbsp. SHORTENING
  1 cup NONFAT PLAIN YOGURT
Sauce:
  1 Tbsp. CANOLA or OLIVE OIL
  6 ounces CHORIZO, crumbled (or diced HAM)
  2 Tbsp. WHOLE-WHEAT or ALL-PURPOSE FLOUR
  2 cups MILK
  1/3 cup chopped, roasted and peeled NEW MEXICO
      GREEN CHILES
  4 EGGS, fried or poached

For the biscuits, in a medium bowl stir together the 1 1/4 cups flour, cornmeal, baking powder, soda and salt. With a fork or pastry cutter, mix in the shortening until it forms a crumbly mixture. Gently stir in the yogurt just to moisten it and form a soft dough. Lightly grease a cookie sheet and preheat the oven to 450 degrees. Place 1" thick and 3" across rounds of the dough onto the prepared cookie sheet, making 4 biscuits. Bake at 450 degrees for 15 minutes.

Meanwhile, in a heavy skillet over medium heat sauté the chorizo in the oil until it's golden, about 7 - 10 minutes. Stir in the 2 Tbsp. of flour and cook, stirring, for 5 minutes. Whisk in the milk and continue stirring until the mixture is smooth and thickens. Stir in the green chiles and season with salt to taste.

To serve, split the biscuits open. Top each with an egg and some of the sauce, as desired.

Yields 4 servings.

Jazz-time Quiche

The old mining town of Madrid, located about 25 miles southwest of Santa Fe, is currently enjoying a renaissance. Artists are lovingly restoring many of the old abandoned homes. On summer weekends, the town comes alive with jazz festivals. This recipe revitalizes an ordinary quiche with chiles, dried tomatoes, onions and olives, creating something quite jazzy, too.

4 ounces soft GOAT CHEESE or BRIE
4 ounces CREAM CHEESE or NEUFCHÂTEL CHEESE
1 1/2 Tbsp. FLOUR
1 1/4 cups LIGHT CREAM or EVAPORATED SKIM MILK
3 EGGS
1/4 cup chopped, roasted and peeled NEW MEXICO
     GREEN CHILES
1/4 cup chopped MARINATED SUNDRIED
     TOMATOES, patted dry
2 Tbsp. finely chopped GREEN ONIONS
1/2 cup SLICED BLACK OLIVES
9-inch PIE CRUST, partially baked at 400 degrees for 10 minutes

In a large bowl, blend together the cheeses, flour, cream and eggs. Stir in the chiles. Sprinkle the sundried tomatoes, green onions and olives on the bottom of the partially baked pie crust. Gently pour the egg mixture over. Cover the edges of the pastry crust with foil. Bake at 400 degrees for 30 minutes until set. Remove pie from oven and let sit 10 minutes before cutting.

Yields one 9" quiche, making 6 servings.

Anasazi Squash Salad

The Southwestern pueblo Indians are believed to be descendants of the Anasazi, or "ancient ones." This main dish salad brings the fresh tastes of their native summer squashes into modern times.

2 medium YELLOW SQUASH or ZUCCHINI
1 cup diced CHICKEN or TURKEY BREAST
2 tsp. LAND OF ENCHANTMENT SPICE MIX (see page 15)
1 Tbsp. OLIVE OIL
1/3 cup chopped MARINATED SUNDRIED
**   TOMATOES, patted dry**
1/2 cup chopped GREEN ONIONS
1/4 cup chopped, roasted and peeled NEW MEXICO
**   GREEN CHILES**
1/3 cup chopped FRESH CILANTRO LEAVES
2 Tbsp. LIME JUICE
2 Tbsp. TEQUILA
SALT to taste
1 cup grated mild GOAT CHEESE or any WHITE CHEESE

Coarsely grate the squash (or zucchini) into a colander, sprinkle lightly with salt, drain 30 minutes and squeeze dry. Reserve. In a small bowl, toss the chicken with the spice mix. Heat the olive oil in a large skillet over medium high heat. Add the chicken pieces and fry, tossing occasionally, until golden. Add the reserved zucchini, tomatoes, green onions and chile. Toss over medium heat until heated through and the zucchini is crisp and tender, about 8 minutes. Toss in the cilantro, lime juice, tequila, salt and cheese. Heat through.

Yields 4 servings.

Wrangler Grilled Beef Salad

A fast and easy steak and salad meal-in-one. Serve it with thick slices of garlic toast.

4 - 6 cups ASSORTED SALAD GREENS
1 small RED ONION, halved and thinly sliced
1/2 medium RED BELL PEPPER, julienned
1/2 cup SLICED BLACK OLIVES
1 TOMATO, wedged
1 AVOCADO, peeled, seeded and sliced
1 Tbsp. LAND OF ENCHANTMENT SPICE MIX (see page 15)
1/2 pound STEAK or LONDON BROIL, trimmed of fat
1 cup CACTUS DRESSING (see page 17)

Arrange the salad greens, red onion, bell pepper, olives, tomato and avocado on serving plates.

Pat the spice mix over the meat and grill over hot coals until medium rare, then cut into julienne strips. Arrange the grilled meat over the salad. Drizzle the dressing generously over all.

Yields 2 generous main dish servings.

Hacienda Pasta

This is a homey dish that assembles quickly. Enjoy it when you want something more special than the usual macaroni casserole dinner.

3/4 cup GREEN CHILE CILANTRO PESTO (see page 14)
1 pound RED POTATOES (about 3 medium potatoes), 1/2-inch dice, boiled tender, drained
8 ounces PENNE or other small PASTA, cooked al dente, drained
3/4 cup SKIM MILK blended with 1 1/2 Tbsp. NON-INSTANT SKIM MILK POWDER
SALT and PEPPER to taste
3 ounces GOAT CHEESE, crumbled

In a large heavyweight saucepan add the pesto, potatoes, pasta and milk. Heat slowly over low heat, stirring occasionally, until hot. Salt and pepper to taste. Toss in the cheese and serve.

Yields 4 servings.

Fireworks Grilled Chicken

This hot, sweet marinade brings out the best in grilled chicken. Leftovers are great for use in pastas and salads.

Marinade:

1 1/2 tsp. PREPARED MUSTARD
2 large GARLIC CLOVES, crushed
1 1/2 Tbsp. SUN CHILE HONEY (see page 98)
1/2 tsp. SALT
1/4 cup ORANGE JUICE
1/4 cup VERMOUTH
1/2 tsp. CHILE CARIBE
1/4 tsp. DRIED THYME
2 tsp. LIME JUICE
2 Tbsp. OLIVE OIL
2 pounds CHICKEN BREASTS, boneless, halved

In a large bowl, whisk all the ingredients together except the chicken. Toss in the chicken to coat it with the marinade. Cover and refrigerate for 1 - 8 hours. Prepare a barbecue grill, preferably with soaked mesquite chips in the coals to contribute their smokey flavor. Grill over a medium hot fire until the chicken is golden on the outside and tender inside, about 7 - 10 minutes per side.

Yields 4 servings.

Sunset Pasta Salad

Any grilled chicken meat will make this salad especially flavorful.

2 cups dry small CURLY or ZITI PASTA, cook al dente, drained
8 ounces cooked CHICKEN or TURKEY BREAST, julienned
1 RED BELL PEPPER, seeded, julienned, cut into 1" lengths
1 TOMATO, diced
1 AVOCADO, peeled, seeded, diced (optional)
1/4 cup toasted PINE NUTS or WALNUTS
1 1/2 cups CACTUS DRESSING (see page 17)

Toss all the ingredients together. Serve over a bed of torn lettuce leaves as a quick and easy main dish salad.

Yields 4 - 6 servings.

Sombrero Frittata

A "sombrero" is a large Mexican hat. Use a large skillet to create a giant sombrero frittata topped with colorful toppings. This spicy egg dish can be served for breakfast, brunch or a late supper.

1 tsp. CANOLA OIL
1/2 cup minced ONION
2 GARLIC CLOVES, minced
1/2 RED BELL PEPPER, diced
4 large EGGS
1/3 cup NONFAT PLAIN YOGURT or MILK
1 Tbsp. chopped FRESH CILANTRO LEAVES
1/4 tsp. CHILE CARIBE
1 TOMATO, seeded, diced
1 AVOCADO, peeled, pitted, diced
1/4 cup chopped, roasted and peeled NEW MEXICO
**   GREEN CHILES**
1/4 cup SLICED BLACK OLIVES
1/2 cup grated CHEESE (your choice)

In a large heavy skillet, heat the oil over medium high heat. Add the onion, garlic and bell pepper. Sauté until the onions soften, about 3 - 5 minutes. Lower the heat to low. In a separate bowl, whisk the eggs, yogurt, cilantro and caribe together. Pour into the skillet. Sprinkle with the tomato, avocado, chiles and olives. Heat without stirring until the bottom half of the eggs set. Sprinkle the cheese on top. Place the skillet under the broiler just until the cheese has melted and is golden. Serve with tomato salsa.

Yields 2 main dish servings.

Escondida Bake

Escondida means "hidden place" in Spanish. Hidden under a crunchy tortilla topping is a rich savory casserole of chorizo, beans, spicy greens and cheese. This dish is sure to not remain a secret for long.

1 pound CHORIZO, sliced
1 tsp. OLIVE OIL
1 small RED ONION, minced
1 pound SPINACH or RUBY CHARD LEAVES, chopped, steamed
    tender, squeezed dry
1 1/2 cup cooked PINTO BEANS, drained
1/2 cup chopped, roasted and peeled NEW MEXICO
    GREEN CHILES
grated LIME ZEST and JUICE of 1/2 LIME
3/4 cup LIGHT CREAM or EVAPORATED MILK
1 EGG
1/2 cup crumbled GOAT CHEESE or BRIE
1 tsp. GROUND CUMIN
1 tsp. DRIED OREGANO
1/2 tsp. CHILE CARIBE
1/2 tsp. SALT
3/4 cup crushed CORN TORTILLA CHIPS
1/2 cup grated PARMESAN or MOZZARELLA CHEESE

In a large skillet over medium high heat, fry the chorizo in the oil until it's golden. Add the onion and sauté for another 3 minutes until the onion is soft. Remove the onion and chorizo to a paper towel to drain.

Preheat the oven to 375 degrees. In a large bowl toss together the chorizo, onions, greens, beans, chile, lime zest and juice, milk, egg, goat (or Brie) cheese and seasonings. Oil a shallow 2-quart baking dish and spoon the mixture into the dish. Toss the corn tortilla chips and Parmesan (or mozzzarella) together and sprinkle on top. Bake at 375 degrees for 30 minutes until golden and bubbling.

Yields 4 servings.

Rio Grande Risotto

Named after the largest river in the state, the Rio Grande, this hardy risotto is sure to satiate your appetite when you want something grand in taste but simple to prepare.

1 Tbsp. OLIVE OIL
1/3 cup finely chopped RED ONION
1/2 medium RED BELL PEPPER, seeded, finely chopped
3 GARLIC CLOVES, minced
1 Tbsp. minced FRESH SAGE (or 1 tsp. crushed dried leaves)
8 ounces CHORIZO, diced
1/2 cup raw ARBORIO or other WHITE RICE
1/4 cup chopped MARINATED SUNDRIED TOMATOES
1/2 cup DRY RED WINE
2 cups STOCK (vegetable, bean, beef or chicken)
2 cups cooked or canned BLACK BEANS, drained
1/2 tsp. GROUND BLACK PEPPER
1/4 cup GREEN CHILE CILANTRO PESTO (see page 14)

In a large heavy saucepan, sauté in oil over medium high heat the onion, bell pepper, garlic, herbs and chorizo until tender. Toss in the rice for 3 minutes to coat. Stir in the tomatoes and lower the heat to maintain an even simmer. While simmering and stirring, gradually add the wine and stock, allowing each addition to disappear before adding next. Add the beans, pepper and pesto and gently heat through. Serve with grated Parmesan or Romano cheese.

Yields 2 main dish or 4 side dish servings.

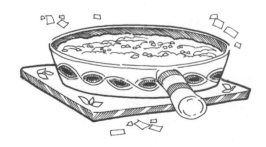

Tequila Chicken

This is an adults-only dish! The rich combination of liquors, oranges and chiles in the sauce permeates every morsel of the chicken. As an entrée, it will create quite a sensation. Serve it with a plain or seasoned rice or pasta to absorb the extra sauce.

1 1/2 tsp. each BUTTER and OIL
1 1/2 pounds boneless, skinless CHICKEN BREASTS (about 4 halves)
1 Tbsp. grated ORANGE ZEST
1 Tbsp. finely chopped GARLIC CLOVES
1 tsp. BEEF STOCK POWDER
2 tsp. TOMATO PASTE
1 Tbsp. FLOUR
1/2 cup TEQUILA
1/4 cup MARSALA or PORT
1/4 cup ORANGE JUICE
1/4 cup rich CHICKEN STOCK
1/2 cup BIG JIM JAM (see page 101)
1/2 tsp. CHILE CARIBE
1 ORANGE, peeled, sliced

In a large heavy skillet, heat the butter and oil over medium high heat. Season the chicken breasts lightly with salt and pepper and add to the skillet. Brown on both sides and remove chicken to a warm plate. Add the orange zest and garlic to the skillet and sauté 2 minutes. Stir in the remaining ingredients. Return the chicken breasts to the skillet and simmer, partially covered, for 30 minutes until the meat is tender and the sauce has thickened to a gravy consistency. After about 20 minutes, check the sauce and if it is too thin, remove the lid and simmer uncovered to reduce liquid. Serve the chicken breasts topped with the sauce.

Yields 2 - 4 servings.

Mixed Sausage and Squash Grill

No one will be able to resist this spicy dish. It cooks in just minutes, making it perfect for entertaining.

**2 each medium ZUCCHINI and YELLOW SQUASH, trimmed
    and cut into 1-inch slices
1/2 large RED ONION, cut into 1-inch sections
1 RED or GOLD BELL PEPPER, seeded, cut into 1-inch sections
1 pound assorted SAUSAGES (Bratwurst, Italian, Kielbasa,
    Linguisa), cut into 1-inch chunks
3/4 cup HOT CILANTRO LIME OIL (see page 16)
4 cups CHICKEN STOCK
1 1/3 cups raw BASMATI or WHITE RICE
SALT and PEPPER to taste**

Skewer alternately the zucchini, yellow squash, onion, bell pepper and sausages on metal kebab sticks. These may be made several hours ahead of time, covered tightly in plastic wrap and held in the refrigerator until needed.

Prepare the grill. Place kebabs about 6 inches over medium coals and grill, brushing generously with the **Hot Cilantro Lime Oil,** until the outsides of the vegetables are golden and the insides are tender, about 15-20 minutes.

Meanwhile, in a medium large saucepan bring the stock to a boil and stir in the rice, salt and pepper. Lower heat to maintain a gentle simmer, cover, and simmer for 15-20 minutes until the liquid has absorbed and the rice is tender. Fluff the rice.

To serve, place the rice onto serving plates and top with the grilled kebabs. Drizzle extra **Hot Cilantro Lime Oil** on top.

Yields 4 servings.

New Mexico Vineyard Dinner

New Mexico wines are ideal accompaniments to local foods. Wine is partnered with lime, regional herbs and meats in this tangy dinner. Serve it over plain rice to soak up the savory sauce.

1 Tbsp. OLIVE OIL
1 1/2 pounds boneless, skinless CHICKEN BREASTS
    (about 4 halves)
8 ounces CHORIZO
3/4 cup chopped, roasted and peeled NEW MEXICO
    GREEN CHILES
2 Tbsp. chopped FRESH SAGE LEAVES (about 15 leaves)
2 1/2 Tbsp. chopped FRESH CILANTRO LEAVES
2 GARLIC CLOVES, crushed
2 Tbsp. LIME JUICE
1 cup DRY WHITE WINE
1/2 cup concentrated CHICKEN STOCK
1/2 medium RED ONION, peeled, thinly sliced
1 tsp. CORNSTARCH dissolved in 1 Tbsp. water
4-6 cups cooked RICE

In a large heavy skillet or dutch oven, add the olive oil and spread it over the bottom of the pan. Cut the chicken and chorizo into 2-inch pieces and place them in the pan. Sprinkle the chiles, sage, cilantro, garlic, lime juice, wine, stock and onion slices over the meat in order. Partially cover the pan and simmer over medium heat for about 45 minutes, until the liquid has reduced by half and the meat tender. Add the dissolved cornstarch and stir until the liquid has thickened to a gravy-like consistency. Serve over the rice.

Yields 4 servings.

Mesa Baskets with Indian Lamb Stew

Lovely baskets woven by many of the native Indians of New Mexico demonstrate their extraordinary talents. These edible baskets capture many flavors traditional in Indian dishes. They will be equally impressive.

Baskets:
- 1 cup BLUE or YELLOW CORNMEAL
- 1 tsp. BAKING POWDER
- 1 cup drained NONFAT PLAIN YOGURT (see page 17)

Filling:
- 1 Tbsp. OLIVE OIL
- 1 ONION, finely chopped
- 2 GARLIC CLOVES, crushed
- 2 cups finely diced or ground LEAN LAMB
- 3/4 cup chopped, roasted and peeled NEW MEXICO GREEN CHILES
- 1/2 cup crumbled soft GOAT CHEESE
- 2 Tbsp. PINE NUTS
- 1 tsp. each minced FRESH ROSEMARY, MINT and OREGANO
- SALT and PEPPER to taste
- 2 Tbsp. SOUR CREAM

To make the baskets, in a small bowl combine the cornmeal, baking powder and yogurt. Grease 5 jumbo nonstick muffin tins. Spoon the cornmeal batter into the prepared tins.

To make the filling, in a heavy skillet over medium high heat, sauté the onion, garlic, and lamb until the lamb is no longer pink. Add the chiles, cheese, nuts, herbs salt and pepper, and sour cream to the skillet and remove from heat. Place spoonfuls of the filling on top of the cornmeal mixtures, dividing equally among the tins. Gently push down on the fillings with a spoon to make the cornmeal mixture come up the sides. Bake in a preheated oven at 350 degrees for 15-20 minutes. Remove from the oven and cool for 5 minutes before removing to serving plates.

Yields 5 jumbo baskets, serving 2 - 4.

Chile Jam'n Kebabs

These spicy kebabs have just the right amount of sweetness and fiery bite. They are almost effortless to prepare yet look and taste quite exquisite.

1 cup BIG JIM JAM (see page 101)
1/2 cup PREPARED SPICY MUSTARD
1/3 cup TEQUILA
2 Tbsp. OLIVE OIL
3 GARLIC CLOVES, crushed
1 tsp. grated LEMON ZEST
1/4 tsp. CAYENNE
1 tsp. SALT
4 pounds boneless, skinless CHICKEN BREASTS, cut into
 1 1/2-inch pieces
BAMBOO SKEWERS

In a small bowl combine the jam, mustard, tequila, oil, garlic, zest, cayenne and salt. This may be made ahead of time and kept, tightly covered, in the refrigerator until needed. Place the chicken pieces in a shallow bowl and toss them with 2/3 of the jam mixture. Cover the bowl and marinate the chicken for at least 1 hour in the refrigerator. Place the bamboo skewers in a tall glass of water to soak for hour while the chicken marinates. Then, skewer the marinated chicken.

Prepare the grill with medium hot coals. Grill the chicken, basting with additional sauce, until the meat is glazed and golden on the outside and tender inside, about 5 - 7 minutes on each side. Serve the kebabs with about 9 cups of cooked plain rice or **New Mexico Herbed Rice** (see page 89).

Yields 6 - 8 servings.

New Mexico Taco Burgers

These aren't your usual mundane cheeseburgers. Vibrantly seasoned with the flavors of the region, they're sure to win rave reviews among chile lovers.

1 1/2 pounds fresh **GROUND LEAN BEEF**
2/3 cup finely chopped **ONION**
3/4 cup chopped, roasted and peeled **NEW MEXICO GREEN CHILES**
1 Tbsp. **NEW MEXICO RED CHILE POWDER**
3 **GARLIC CLOVES**, finely chopped
1 tsp. **GROUND CUMIN**
1 tsp. **CAYENNE**
1 tsp. **SALT**
1/2 cup **AUTHENTIC NEW MEXICO RED CHILE SAUCE** (see page 13)
1 cup shredded **SHARP CHEDDAR CHEESE**
6 slices **PECOS TRAIL CORNBREAD** (see page 94)

Toppings:
  TACO SAUCE
  CHEDDAR SLICES
  AVOCADO SLICES
  DICED TOMATO
  NEW MEXICO SOUR CREAM DIP (see page 18)

In a large bowl, combine the beef, onion, chiles, chile powder, garlic, cumin, cayenne, salt, chile sauce and 1 cup shredded sharp cheddar together, mixing gently. Form into 6 patties. Place over a hot grill for about 6 minutes per side, until browned and meat has cooked through until no longer pink in the center. Place slices of cheddar on top of the burgers, if desired, then cover the grill and heat just until the cheese has melted. Place the burgers on toasted cornbread slices. Top with additional taco or enchilada sauce, slices of avocado and tomatoes and the *New Mexico Sour Cream Dip* as desired.

Yields 6 servings.

Green Chile Mock Moussaka

Although rich in chile flavor, this dish will remind you of Greek moussaka. It can be made several hours before baking and kept, tightly covered, in the refrigerator. For a more substantial main dish, layer 8 ounces of thinly sliced cooked turkey or chicken breast or 4 hard boiled eggs with the vegetables.

Sauce:
- 1/2 ONION, chopped
- 3 GARLIC CLOVES, crushed
- 1 Tbsp. CANOLA or OLIVE OIL
- 1 heaping cup chopped, roasted and peeled NEW MEXICO GREEN CHILES
- 2 cups CHICKEN STOCK
- 2 Tbsp. chopped FRESH CILANTRO LEAVES
- 1 tsp. DRIED OREGANO
- 2 heaping Tbsp. CORN MASA HARINA MIX

Vegetables:
- 1 large BAKING POTATO (12 ounces), thinly sliced lengthwise
- 1 large EGGPLANT (about 1 1/2 pounds), peeled, 1/3-inch lengthwise slices
- 2 Tbsp. OLIVE OIL for brushing onto vegetables
- 3/4 tsp. SALT
- 1/4 tsp. GROUND BLACK PEPPER
- 1/4 tsp. GRANULATED GARLIC
- 1/4 tsp. GROUND CUMIN
- 6 ounces CHEESE (mozzarella, fontina, Gouda, cheddar or any mild cheese), grated

For the sauce, in a heavy saucepan over medium high heat sauté the onion and garlic in the oil until tender, about 3 minutes. Add the chiles, stock, cilantro and oregano and heat to boiling. Dissolve the masa in 1/4 cup of water and stir into the sauce. Simmer, stirring, for 3-4 minutes until slightly thickened.

To prepare the vegetables, oil a baking sheet with olive oil. Place the potato and eggplant slices on the prepared sheet and lightly brush them with oil. In a tiny bowl, toss together the salt, pepper, garlic and cumin. Sprinkle the vegetable slices lightly with the

(Continued on next page)

(Continued from previous page)

seasoned salt. Broil until golden and lightly crisp. Turn, brush again with oil and sprinkle with additional seasoned salt. Broil until the second side is golden and lightly crisp.

To assemble, lightly oil a 9-inch glass baking dish and layer the potatoes, half the sauce, half the cheese, the eggplant, the balance of the sauce and the rest of the cheese.

When ready to serve, preheat the oven to 350 degrees. Bake the casserole at 350 degrees for 45 minutes until bubbling and the cheese is golden.

Yields 4 servings.

Casa Posole and Cheese

This is a homey family dish. It will remind you of the macaroni and cheese of your youth, but with the chewiness and flavor found only in posole. The skim milk is blended with milk powder and some of the posole to lend creaminess without adding fat.

1 1/2 tsp. CANOLA OIL
1/4 cup finely chopped ONIONS
2 GARLIC CLOVES, minced
3 1/2 cups cooked POSOLE, divided (see page 49)
2/3 cup SKIM MILK
2 Tbsp. NON-INSTANT SKIM MILK POWDER
1/2 cup chopped, roasted and peeled NEW MEXICO
**   GREEN CHILES**
SALT and PEPPER to taste
1/2 cup grated mild WHITE CHEESE of choice

In a large heavy saucepan, heat the oil over medium high heat and sauté the onions and garlic until softened, about 3 minutes. In a blender place 2 cups of the posole, the milk and milk powder and partially purée. Add to the pot with the rest of the whole posole, green chiles and seasonings to taste. Cook over medium heat until heated through, stirring occasionally. Stir in the cheese just until melted and serve.

Yields 4 servings.

Watercolor Mesas

Across New Mexico are large land tables composed of multiple layers of colorful rocks topped with green vegetation. This dish is composed of colorful tasty layers frosted with a vibrant green pesto. It will bring a touch of our picture perfect mesas to your table.

3 Tbsp. OLIVE OIL
2 GARLIC CLOVES, crushed or 1/2 tsp. GRANULATED GARLIC
1 pound POTATOES, thinly sliced
SALT and PEPPER to taste
1/2 cup crumbled GOAT CHEESE
1/4 cup SLICED BLACK OLIVES
3 Tbsp. chopped MARINATED SUNDRIED TOMATOES, drained
1 pound boneless WHITE FISH FILLETS (such as red snapper, cod,
   orange roughy)
1/2 cup GREEN CHILE CILANTRO PESTO (see page 14)

In a large, heavy, ovenproof skillet, heat the olive oil over medium high heat. Add the garlic and sauté one minute. Add the potato slices and fry, turning occasionally, until the potatoes are golden on both sides.

Season the potato slices with salt and pepper and arrange them in a slightly overlapping pattern on the bottom of the skillet. Sprinkle with the cheese, black olives and dried tomatoes. Place the fish fillets on top and spoon the pesto generously over the fillets to cover them. Place the skillet about 8 inches under a broiler until the fillets are flaky and the cheese is softened.

This dish can be prepared ahead of time and stored, covered, in the refrigerator. To cook the chilled dish, it works best to place it in a preheated 400 degree oven for about 20 - 30 minutes until everything is heated through and the fillets are flaky.

Yields 2 - 4 servings.

Baked Chile Rellenos in Clouds

Chile rellenos are popular here, especially in restaurants. Traditional rellenos are made by stuffing mild meaty green chiles with a savory filling, dipping them in a batter and deep frying until the coating is crispy. They are messy and too time consuming for many home cooks.

This baked version is much easier to make and much lower in fat. It still manages to capture the best attributes of chile rellenos - a fluffy, crispy coating surrounding succulent chiles stuffed with melting cheese and meat. Serve this dish with guacamole, salsa, olives, sour cream and chopped green onions, as desired, for the full effect.

8-12 roasted and peeled BIG JIM GREEN CHILES
8 ounces CHEESE of choice, cut into long 1/4-inch thick finger-
**   shaped slices**
8 ounces cooked TURKEY or CHICKEN, julienned, optional
1/2 cup chopped ONIONS sautéed tender in 1 tsp. oil
3 EGG YOLKS
3/4 cup MILK
3/4 cup WHOLE-WHEAT or ALL-PURPOSE FLOUR
1/2 tsp. SALT
3 EGG WHITES, beaten to soft peaks

Place a cheese finger and small amount of meat in each of the chiles. Lightly oil a 9-inch baking dish and arrange the stuffed chiles in one or two layers. Strew the sautéed onions on top. Alternately, slice the chiles to open them flat. Arrange half of the chiles in one layer on the bottom of the prepared dish, top with a layer of cheese, and meat if desired, and top with the remaining chiles. Sprinkle the sautéed onions on top.

Preheat the oven to 350 degrees. In a separate bowl, blend the yolks, milk, flour and salt together. Fold in the beaten egg whites and spread the mixture over the casserole. Bake at 350 degrees for 25 minutes until golden.

Yields 4 servings.

Zia Strata

Zia, the Pueblo Indians' symbol for the sun, is also the state insignia. Remember the sun when making this uniquely New Mexican strata. Prepare it at sunset, because it must sit overnight in the refrigerator. Then, bake it at sunrise the following morning.

5-6 one-inch slices PECOS TRAIL CORNBREAD (see page 94)
4 ounces SHARP CHEDDAR CHEESE, shredded
8 ounces CHORIZO, casings removed, crumbled, browned and
    drained on paper towels
1/4 cup finely chopped ONION
1/2 cup chopped, roasted and peeled NEW MEXICO
    GREEN CHILES
3 EGGS
1 2/3 cups MILK
1 1/2 tsp. PREPARED MUSTARD
1/4 tsp. GROUND CUMIN
1/4 tsp. GROUND BLACK PEPPER

Butter a 1 1/2 quart soufflé dish. Alternately layer the bread, cheddar, chorizo, onions and chiles to form 2 layers of each. In a small bowl, whisk the eggs, milk, mustard, cumin and pepper together. Gently pour over the layers. Cover the dish and refrigerate it for six to ten hours.

Preheat the oven to 350 degrees and remove the dish from the refrigerator. Bake at 350 degrees for 45 minutes until it is puffed and golden.

Yields 2 main dish or 4 side dish servings.

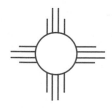

Grilled Nambe Chicken Rolls

The Nambe Pueblo is tucked among cottonwood trees north of Santa Fe. The quiet residents of this pueblo were named Nambe which means "people of the rounded earth." These chicken rolls are simple to prepare. They may be made in the morning and refrigerated until ready for a quick grilling.

1 1/2 pounds boneless, skinless CHICKEN BREASTS
    (about 2 whole breasts)
1/2 cup GREEN CHILE CILANTRO PESTO (see page 14)
1 RED BELL PEPPER, roasted, peeled and julienned
2 Tbsp. VERMOUTH
2 Tbsp. LIME JUICE
2 Tbsp. OLIVE OIL
1/4 tsp. SALT
1/4 tsp. GROUND BLACK PEPPER
CILANTRO LIME RICE (see page 83)

Cut the whole chicken breasts in half and place them between sheets of plastic wrap. Pound until the chicken has flattened to a thickness of about 1/2-inch. Spread each breast half with 2 tablespoons of the pesto and arrange 1/4 of the red bell pepper slivers on top. Roll up and secure with toothpicks. Wrap the rolls tightly in plastic wrap and store them in the refrigerator for up to 8 hours before cooking.

Prepare the barbecue grill. In a small bowl or cup, toss together the vermouth, lime juice, olive oil , salt and pepper. Grill the chicken rolls about 6 inches above hot coals, basting with the dressing until the outsides are golden and the chicken is no longer pink inside. Alternately, the chicken rolls may be placed under a broiler, basting and turning, until done. Serve these tasty rolls nested in *Cilantro Lime Rice.*

Yields 4 servings.

Navajo Blanket Pizza

An artistic tapestry of colorful vegetables and golden cheeses is woven as this pizza bakes. Unlike the handmade Indian blankets that are perfectly crafted only after years of experience, you can make this pizza effortlessly in just minutes.

14-inch unbaked PIZZA CRUST (see below)
Toppings:
> 1 cup **GREEN CHILE CILANTRO PESTO** (see page 14)
> 1/2 **RED ONION**, halved, thinly sliced
> 1 **RED** or **GOLD BELL PEPPER**, seeded, julienned
> 3 **ROMA TOMATOES**, seeded and sliced (or 1/4 cup sliced
>   **MARINATED SUNDRIED TOMATOES**, patted dry)
> 1/2 cup **SLICED BLACK OLIVES**
> 4-6 ounces **ARTICHOKE HEARTS**, marinated or canned, drained
>   and halved
> 4-6 ounces **GOAT CHEESE, BRIE** or **MOZZARELLA**, grated
> 1/4 cup freshly grated **PARMESAN** or **ROMANO CHEESE**

Preheat the oven to 475 degrees and lightly brush a large baking or cookie sheet with olive oil. Place the unbaked pizza crust on the baking sheet. Spread evenly with the pesto and arrange the toppings on top, in the order shown. Bake at 475 degrees for 12-15 minutes until the crust is golden and the toppings hot.

Yields about 4 servings.

Pizza Crust

1 cup **WARM WATER**
1 Tbsp. **ACTIVE DRY YEAST**
pinch **SUGAR**
2 Tbsp. **OLIVE OIL**
1/2 tsp. **SALT**

2 3/4 cups **WHOLE-WHEAT BREAD
   FLOUR**
1/4 cup **GLUTEN FLOUR** (or replace
   with **WHOLE-WHEAT**)

In a medium bowl, dissolve the yeast in the sugar and warm water. Stir in the oil, salt, and half of the flour. Beat for several minutes until stringy. Gradually mix in the rest of the flour and knead on a floured surface until the dough is smooth and soft, about 10 minutes Place on the olive oil-coated baking sheet. Cover and let rise in warm moist place until doubled. Pat or roll out to desired size and then proceed with the recipe above.

Thunder Subs

Late afternoon thunderstorms are welcomed by New Mexicans for the cooling rains they bring during the summer months. These meatless submarine sandwiches will be equally appreciated at your house, but more for their spicy heat and succulent flavors. By lightly brushing the eggplant and onion slices with garlic oil and broiling them, they become quite tender without absorbing much grease.

1 EGGPLANT (about 1 1/2 pounds), peeled, cut into 1/3-inch lengthwise slices
4 Tbsp. OLIVE OIL with 1 tsp. GRANULATED GARLIC
1 small RED ONION, 1/4-inch slices
4 thick slices WHOLEGRAIN or FRENCH BREAD (each slice should measure about 4 x 5 inches around and 1-inch thick)
6 ounces SMOKED CHEESE (Gouda, mozzarella or provolone), sliced
3 Tbsp. chopped, roasted and peeled NEW MEXICO GREEN CHILES
1 1/2 cups torn LETTUCE, CHARD or SPINACH LEAVES
1 TOMATO, sliced
3 Tbsp. SANDSTONE MAYONNAISE (see page 15)

Brush the eggplant slices with the garlic oil and place them in a single layer on a cookie sheet. Place them under the broiler until the tops are golden. Turn the slices over and brush with more of the oil. Top with the red onion slices and brush them lightly with the garlic oil. Sprinkle lightly with ground black pepper. Continue to broil until the second sides are golden and the vegetables are tender.

Layer on 2 slices of the bread the eggplant, onions, and smoked cheese. Top with the chiles, lettuce and tomato. Spread the last 2 slices of bread generously with the mayonnaise and place on top of the fillings. Wrap the sandwiches in foil and bake (or wrap in plastic wrap and microwave) until the bread is hot and the cheese is melting.

Yields 2 sandwiches for 2 people impersonating Dagwood.

La Huerta Pasta

Named after a Spanish garden, this pasta is resplendent with the fresh vegetables from a late summer New Mexico garden. Although it is fast and easy to assemble, it will delight your most special guests.

3/4 cup GREEN CHILE CILANTRO PESTO (see page14)
1 pound PASTA (plain or cilantro, lemon, or spinach flavor),
   boiled in salted water until al dente, drained

Toppings:
   1 RED or GOLD BELL PEPPER, roasted, peeled, julienned
   3 cups sliced VEGETABLES (zucchini, yellow squash, red onion
      and/or peeled eggplant), grilled while basting with a
      vinaigrette dressing or 2 cups grilled spicy CHICKEN MEAT,
      julienned
   3 Tbsp. lightly toasted PINE NUTS
   2 ROMA TOMATOES, seeded, diced (or 1/4 cup chopped
      MARINATED SUNDRIED TOMATOES, drained)
   1/2 cup sliced BLACK OLIVES
   4 ounces BRIE, diced
   1/2 cup grated PARMESAN or ROMANO cheese

In the pasta cooking pot, toss the pesto with the drained pasta over medium heat just to heat through. Place on four serving plates and sprinkle a variety of the topping choices over each.

Yields 4 servings.

SIDE DISHES

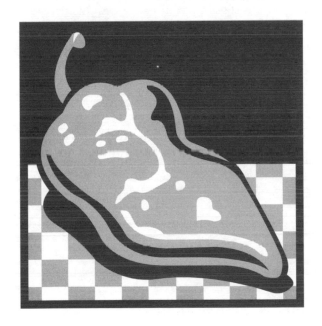

Anasazi Beans

All types of pinto beans have been a dietary staple in New Mexico for thousands of years. Anasazi beans are especially colorful beans speckled with red and white. Nowadays, most New Mexicans still enjoy them with any meal of the day. Be sure to make plenty because they will keep well for up to 5 days in the refrigerator and can be frozen for up to 6 months.

**1 pound (2 1/2 cups) dried ANASAZI BEANS soaked overnight
   and drained (pinto beans may be substituted)**
3/4 cup CHICOS (dried corn), soaked overnight, drained, optional
1 ONION, finely chopped
3 GARLIC CLOVES, minced
2 tsp. CHILE CARIBE
1 tsp. GROUND CUMIN

Place all of the ingredients in a large heavy saucepan and add water to come up 2 inches above the beans. Partially cover the saucepan and simmer over medium low heat for 2 - 4 hours until tender. Watch carefully as they may need more water. Alternately you may place the ingredients and water in a crock pot and cook covered for 6-8 hours unattended until the beans are tender. Season to taste with salt.

Yields about 9 cups with the chicos, 6 1/2 cups without.

Chicos are a special variety of dried corn used throughout Northern New Mexico. They are usually dried in an Indian adobe "horno" oven and have a unique smokey flavor and aroma. They are scarce, but available at specialty stores. New Mexicans rarely cook their pinto beans without throwing in a handful of chicos for flavor.

Miner's Hash Browns

Try these spicy hashbrowns with breakfast eggs. Serve with tomato salsa and warm flour tortillas.

1 Tbsp. CANOLA OIL
3 GARLIC CLOVES, minced
1/2 cup finely chopped ONION
1/2 cup finely diced RED BELL PEPPER
1 large BAKING POTATO (about 12 ounces), boiled tender, diced
1/4 cup chopped, roasted and peeled NEW MEXICO GREEN
   CHILES or 1 tsp. CHILE CARIBE
1/4 cup chopped FRESH CILANTRO LEAVES
1/4 cup crumbled fried BACON or CHORIZO (or 2 Tbsp. IMITATION
   BACON BITS)
1/4 tsp. SALT or to taste

In a large heavy skillet over medium high heat, heat the oil and add the garlic, onion, bell pepper, and potatoes. Fry, stirring, until the potatoes are lightly golden and the onions are tender, about 8 minutes. Stir in the chiles, cilantro and bacon. Heat through. Salt to taste and serve.

Yields 4 servings.

Cilantro Lime Rice

Lime, cilantro and chiles are natural partners. When stirred into rice, the rice takes on a pleasant tanginess that is ideal with grilled meats.

2 cups CHICKEN STOCK
1 cup raw BASMATI or other WHITE RICE
SALT and PEPPER to taste
1/4 cup HOT CILANTRO LIME OIL (see page 16)
3 GREEN ONIONS, chopped (about 1/3 cup)

In a medium saucepan bring the stock to a simmer. Stir in the rice, salt and pepper. Cover the pan and lower the heat to maintain a gentle simmer until the rice is tender and the liquid has been absorbed, about 20 minutes. Fluff and stir in the oil and onions. Garnish with additional lime slices.

Yields about 3 1/2 cups, serving 2 - 4.

Enchanted Vegetables

In just minutes, this recipe will turn any ordinary vegetable into something truly irresistible. This dish can be successfully made on the stovetop or in the microwave.

**3 cups BROCCOLI or CAULIFLOWER FLOWERETS (or sliced
     CARROTS, or 12 cups chopped CHARD or SPINACH LEAVES)**
2 Tbsp. of rich STOCK (chicken, beef or vegetable)
2 tsp. LAND OF ENCHANTMENT SPICE MIX (see page 15)
1/2 cup grated CHEESE of choice
2 Tbsp. coarsely chopped PECANS

In a large covered saucepan over medium heat, steam the vegetables in the stock just until they are crisp tender. In a small bowl toss together the spice mix, cheese and pecans. Sprinkle the mixture over the vegetables and heat just to melt the spiced cheese into the vegetables.

Yields 3 - 4 servings

Lightning Strike Roasted Potatoes

For your next outdoor meal, try these savory potato spears. They make delightful alternatives to the usual potato salad.

3 medium BAKING POTATOES (about 8 ounces each)
1/2 cup CHILE CUMIN OIL (see page 16)

Cut each potato lengthwise into fourths, making spears. Place them in a microwave-proof dish with 1/4 cup water on the bottom. Cover and microwave until the potatoes are almost tender. Drain. Alternately, you may boil or steam the potatoes until they're almost tender.

Cut heavy duty foil into three 1-foot long pieces. Place 4 potato spears onto each piece of foil. Drizzle the oil over the potatoes. Fold the foil over the potatoes and pinch to seal, creating 3 bundles. Place them over a medium hot grill or bake in a 350 degree oven for about 20-30 minutes, until heated through.

Yields 3 servings.

Watercolor Pasta Salad

New Mexico landscapes are a treasure for watercolor artists. This simple salad is vibrant with oranges contrasted with black olives and deep green spinach against the creamy beans and pasta.

Dressing:
>   2 Tbsp. ORANGE JUICE CONCENTRATE
>   grated RIND of 1 ORANGE
>   2 Tbsp. RED WINE VINEGAR
>   2 GARLIC CLOVES, crushed
>   3 Tbsp. OLIVE OIL
>   1/4 tsp. CHILI CARIBE
>   1/4 tsp. SALT

8 ounces SMALL PASTA, cooked al dente, drained
1 ORANGE, peeled, diced
1 1/4 cups cooked GARBANZO BEANS or WHITE BEANS
1 cup SLICED BLACK OLIVES
1/2 cup WALNUT HALVES, toasted
1 bunch SPINACH LEAVES (8 ounces), torn

In a large bowl, whisk the dressing ingredients together. Toss the remaining ingredients into the dressing. Serve immediately or keep in the refrigerator for up to 4 hours, tightly covered.

Yields 4 side dish servings.

Roasted Chile Corn

Planning a barbecue? These corn bundles can be prepared in minutes. They make the perfect accompaniments to any outdoor meal.

4 ears of CORN ON THE COB, husked
1/2 cup CHILE CUMIN OIL (see page 16)

Cut four pieces of heavy duty foil into 15 inch-long squares. Place an ear of corn onto each piece of foil. Drizzle a fourth of the oil over each ear of corn. Fold the foil over and pinch to seal the edges, forming 4 bundles. Place the foil packets over a medium hot grill or bake in a 350 degree oven until they're hot to touch and the oil can be heard sizzling, about 20 minutes.

Yields 4 servings.

New Mexican Cottontail Salad

Carrots become more than bunny food in this refreshing salad with a touch of New Mexico in every bite.

1 pound CARROTS, shredded
1/4 cup chopped DRIED APRICOTS
1/2 cup diced, seeded CUCUMBER, or whole SEEDLESS
    GREEN GRAPES
3 Tbsp. LEMON JUICE
2 Tbsp. OLIVE OIL
2 GARLIC CLOVES, crushed
2 tsp. HONEY
1/2 tsp. GROUND CUMIN
1/2 tsp. NEW MEXICO RED CHILE POWDER
1 Tbsp. finely chopped MINT LEAVES
SALT and PEPPER to taste

In a large bowl, toss all of the ingredients together. Serve immediately or cover tightly and keep it in the refrigerator for up to 6 hours before serving.

Yields 6 - 8 servings.

Conchas Salad

For a simple pasta salad that can be made hours before you need it, this is perfect. To make it truly outstanding, add leftover grilled chicken or smoked chicken. Use shell-shaped pasta in honor of the Spanish word "conchas" for shell.

1 1/2 cups CONQUISTADOR GREEN OLIVE SALSA (see page 34)
2 cups small CURLY or SHELL PASTA, boiled in salted
    water until al dente, drained
1/3 cup minced RED ONION
8 ounces cooked, grilled or smoked skinless CHICKEN or TURKEY
    BREAST, julienned
8 ROMAINE LETTUCE LEAVES, trimmed, torn

In a large bowl, toss all of the ingredients together. Cover and chill in the refrigerator for several hours until serving.

Yields 4 servings.

Mardi Gras Rice

Mardi Gras celebrations in early February are characterized by vivid colors and zesty foods. This rice is a party in every bite.

2 1/2 cups MEAT or VEGETABLE STOCK
1 cup raw WHITE RICE
1 Tbsp. CANOLA OIL
1/2 cup , finely chopped RED or YELLOW ONION
1/2 cup each, finely chopped, seeded RED and GREEN BELL
    PEPPER
3 GARLIC CLOVES, crushed
1/4 cup chopped, roasted and peeled NEW MEXICO
    GREEN CHILES
1 TOMATO, seeded, diced
1/4 cup chopped GREEN OLIVES
JUICE and grated ZEST of 1 LIME
1/4 cup chopped FRESH CILANTRO LEAVES
1/2 cup CORN KERNELS (fresh or frozen)
SALT and PEPPER to taste

In a medium saucepan bring the stock to a simmer. Stir in the rice. Cover and lower the heat to maintain a gentle simmer until the rice is tender and the liquid has been absorbed, about 20 minutes.

Meanwhile in a heavy skillet heat the oil over medium high heat and fry the onion, bell peppers and garlic until they are tender, about 5 minutes. Toss in the chiles, tomato, olives, lime zest and juice, cilantro and corn. Lower the heat and sauté a few more minutes until the ingredients have heated through.

Fluff the rice and toss it into the skillet mixture. Season to taste with salt and pepper.

Yields 4 servings.

Hondo Bake

This is a simple lowfat gratin without the cheese. By baking the potatoes and onions in a spicy milk, they absorb its rich flavors and meld into the thick gravy. Serve this alongside any grilled meat. It's pure ambrosia for any meat and potato lover.

**1 pound POTATOES (about 2 medium), halved and cut
    into 1/4-inch thick slices**
1 small ONION, quartered and cut into 1/4-inch thick slices
1 cup MILK
1 cup CONCENTRATED CHICKEN STOCK
2 Tbsp. NEW MEXICO RED CHILE POWDER
1 tsp. GROUND CUMIN
1 tsp. DRIED OREGANO
3 GARLIC CLOVES, crushed
SALT and PEPPER to taste

Preheat the oven to 400 degrees. Butter a deep 1 1/2 quart baking dish. Layer in the prepared dish the potatoes and onions. Blend the remaining ingredients together and pour over the layers. Cover the dish and bake at 400 degrees for 45 minutes. Remove the cover, toss, and bake an additional 25 minutes, until the potatoes are tender and the liquid has reduced to a thick gravy.

Yields 4 servings.

New Mexico Herbed Rice

Stimulated with chiles, lemon and fresh herbs, this rice makes a lovely accompaniment to grilled chicken and seafood.

3 cups RICH CHICKEN STOCK
1 1/3 cups raw WHITE RICE
1/4 cup chopped, roasted and peeled NEW MEXICO
  GREEN CHILES
1/4 tsp. each of SALT and PEPPER
1 1/2 tsp. LEMON ZEST
1 Tbsp. each chopped FRESH CHIVES, PARSLEY and CILANTRO

In a medium saucepan bring the stock to a simmer. Stir in the rice, chile, salt and pepper. Cover and lower the heat to maintain a gentle simmer until the rice is tender and the liquid has been absorbed, about 20 minutes. Fluff and stir in the lemon zest and herbs.

Yields about 4 cups, serving 4.

Calabacitas con Crema

Every New Mexican family has their own version of this popular summer side dish. What every recipe has in common is squash cooked with chiles. This version is enriched with cream and traditional herbs. Feel free to add fresh corn kernels as they are common additions for this dish.

3/4 pound ZUCCHINI, diced
1 TOMATO, chopped
SALT and PEPPER to taste
2 Tbsp. minced FRESH CILANTRO LEAVES
2 GARLIC CLOVES, minced
1 Tbsp. minced FRESH MINT LEAVES
3/4 tsp. GROUND CINNAMON
1/3 cup chopped, roasted and peeled NEW MEXICO
**   GREEN CHILES**
1/4 cup LIGHT CREAM

In a large heavy saucepan stir all of the ingredients together. Place over low heat and simmer, covered, until the zucchini is tender and the sauce is creamy, about 30 minutes.

Yields 2 to 4 side dish servings.

BAKED GOODS

Miniature Diablo Muffins

These little "devilishly" spicy bites of a moist savory cake are fun to serve with soups and salads. They also make a nice change of pace from the usual toast or tortillas with eggs. These muffins are best when served warm from the oven, but they will keep well for several days.

1 cup CORNMEAL
1 cup WHOLE-WHEAT PASTRY or ALL-PURPOSE FLOUR
2 tsp. BAKING POWDER
1 1/2 tsp. LAND OF ENCHANTMENT SPICE MIX (see page 15)
1/4 cup minced ONION
1 Tbsp. each minced RED and GREEN BELL PEPPER
4 ounces SHARP CHEDDAR CHEESE, grated
1 cup cooked CORN KERNELS, patted dry (fresh or frozen)
2 large EGGS
1 1/2 cups NONFAT PLAIN YOGURT
1 Tbsp. HONEY

Preheat the oven to 375 degrees. In a large bowl, stir together the cornmeal, flour, baking powder, spice, onion, bell pepper, cheese and corn. In a separate container, whisk the eggs, yogurt and honey together until smooth and gently stir into the dry ingredients just to combine. Grease 30 miniature muffin tins. Fill them 3/4 full and bake at 375 degrees for 12 minutes until the muffins are puffed and lightly bounce back when touched.

Yields 30 miniature muffins.

Real New Mexico Chile

Railroad Stop Biscuits

Biscuits aren't traditional here, but they were popular among travellers passing through on the Santa Fe Railroad. This version will definitely remind you that you're in New Mexico. Like all biscuits, they can be made in minutes and are at their best when served warm from the oven.

1 1/4 cups WHOLE-WHEAT PASTRY or ALL-PURPOSE FLOUR
1/2 cup shredded SHARP CHEDDAR CHEESE
1 Tbsp. SUGAR
1 tsp. NEW MEXICO RED CHILE POWDER
1/2 tsp. BAKING POWDER
1/4 tsp. BAKING SODA
1/4 cup SHORTENING
1 1/2 tsp. ACTIVE YEAST dissolved in 1 Tbsp. warm water
1/4 cup BEER
1/4 cup NONFAT PLAIN YOGURT

Grease a nonstick cookie sheet and preheat the oven to 400 degrees. In a large bowl, place the flour, cheddar, sugar, chile powder, baking powder, soda, and shortening. Cut with a pastry cutter or fork until the mixture is crumbly. In a separate bowl or cup, stir together the yeast mixture, beer and yogurt. Gently add to the flour mixture just until a soft dough forms. Drop 1/4 cup amounts onto the greased cookie sheet, forming 4 - 6 mounds. Bake at 400 degrees for about 15 minutes until they are lightly golden.

Yields 4 to 6 biscuits.

Pecos Trail Cornbread

This fragrant yeast bread is invigorated with a bit of green chile for flavor and cornmeal for crunch. It's wonderful for cheese sandwiches, for toast with breakfast eggs or alongside soups and salads.

3/4 cup WARM WATER
3 Tbsp. HONEY
1 1/2 tsp. ACTIVE DRY YEAST
2 Tbsp. MELTED BUTTER
1/4 cup GLUTEN FLOUR, optional (may substitute BREAD FLOUR)
1 cup WHOLE-WHEAT BREAD FLOUR
1/3 cup CORNMEAL
1/2 tsp. SALT
1/4 cup chopped, roasted and peeled NEW MEXICO
**   GREEN CHILES**
about 1 cup additional FLOUR as needed

In a large bowl dissolve the yeast in the water and honey. Stir in the butter then the gluten flour, 1 cup of the bread flour, cornmeal and salt. Mix with a mixer until it thickens to a spongy consistency. Stir in the chiles. By hand, knead in just enough additional flour to form a soft dough. Knead on a lightly floured surface until it is smooth and elastic, about 15 minutes. Place in a buttered bowl, turn, cover with a warm wet towel and set the bowl in a warm place to rise. Butter a 9 x 5-inch bread pan. When the bread has doubled, punch it down and place it in the prepared pan. Cover it again with the wet towel, return it to a warm place and let it rise until almost doubled. While rising the second time preheat the oven to 375 degrees. Bake at 375 degrees for about 30 minutes until the loaf sounds hollow when tapped. Check it after 20 minutes and cover with a tent of foil if the bread is browning sufficiently. Remove the bread to a rack to cool.

Yields one loaf of bread.

Pineapple Mesa Muffins

Green chiles perfectly complement the sweetness of pineapple. These giant moist muffins make wonderful breakfast or brunch treats.

1/4 cup BUTTER
1/4 cup CANOLA OIL
1 cup SUGAR
2 large EGGS
1 tsp. VANILLA
3 cups WHOLE-WHEAT PASTRY or ALL-PURPOSE FLOUR
1/2 tsp. SALT
1 Tbsp. BAKING POWDER
15 ounce can PINEAPPLE CHUNKS in juice, undrained
1/2 cup chopped, roasted and peeled NEW MEXICO
    GREEN CHILES
2-3 Tbsp. NONFAT PLAIN YOGURT, as needed

Preheat the oven to 400 degrees.

In a large bowl beat together the butter, oil and sugar. Beat in the eggs and vanilla. In another bowl, stir together the flour, salt and baking powder and gently stir into the creamed mixture. Stir in the pineapple and juice, chiles and just enough yogurt to make a spoonable batter.

Grease 10 Jumbo-sized muffin cups and divide batter among them, filling each cup to about 3/4 full. Sprinkle each muffin with an additional 1/2 tsp. of sugar. Bake at 400 degrees for about 20 minutes until the muffins test done (they will spring back when touched or a toothpick inserted into the center will come out clean). Cool 5 minutes in the pan then remove to a rack to cool.

Yields 10 jumbo muffins.

Sun Kissed Honey Scones

*These are buttery rich golden scones kissed with just a hint of chile. Serve them with additional **Sun Chile Honey** for a lovely breakfast treat.*

2 cups WHOLE-WHEAT PASTRY or ALL-PURPOSE FLOUR
1 Tbsp. BAKING POWDER
1/2 tsp. SALT
1/2 cup BUTTER
1/3 cup GOLDEN RAISINS
2 large EGGS
3 Tbsp. SUN CHILE HONEY (see page 98)
1/4 cup NONFAT PLAIN YOGURT, plus more as needed

Preheat the oven to 450 degrees. In a large bowl, stir together the flour, baking powder and salt. Cut in the butter using a fork or pastry cutter until coarse crumbs form. Toss in the raisins. In a small bowl blend the eggs, honey and 1/4 cup yogurt together. Gently mix the blended egg mixture into the crumb mixture, adding about another 1/4 cup yogurt as needed to make a sticky dough. Pat the dough out on a lightly floured counter to form a 1-inch thick square and cut it into 8 smaller squares. Butter a cookie sheet and place the 8 squares on top, allowing 2 inches of space between them. Bake at 450 degrees for 10-12 minutes until they are lightly golden.

Yields 8 scones.

FIERY SWEETS

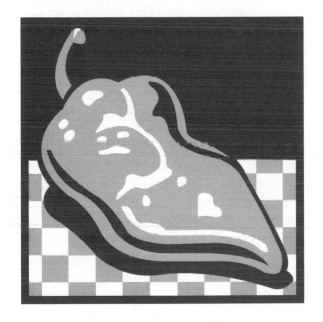

Sun Chile Honey

This honey is infused with red chile peppers, giving it a distinctive flavor and a lovely red hue. It will keep indefinitely in a tightly sealed glass jar. This spiced honey is perfect on warm fresh bread, flour tortillas or sopaipillas.

4 dried NEW MEXICO RED CHILE PEPPERS
2 cups HONEY
CAYENNE to taste

Remove the stems from the chiles and lightly crumble both the peppers and their seeds. Place them in a clean jar with the honey. Place the jar in a sunny window for a week. Taste and if more hotness is desired, add pinches of cayenne. Strain the honey through a fine mesh colander and return to the jar. Place a dried, small whole chile in the jar for decoration.

Yields 2 cups.

Sopaipillas are leavened dough squares deep fried until they puff up like pillows. New Mexicans enjoy them filled with honey or stuffed like pockets with savory fillings.

Atomic Cake

A succulent citrus cake with a kick of spice. It's moist with a citrus and rum-honey syrup and will keep up to a week, tightly covered.

1 cup BUTTER
1 cup SUGAR
3 large EGGS
grated ZEST of 2 large ORANGES
grated ZEST of 1 LEMON
2 1/2 cups sifted WHOLE-WHEAT PASTRY or ALL-PURPOSE FLOUR
2 tsp. BAKING POWDER
1 tsp. BAKING SODA
1/2 tsp. SALT
1 Tbsp. ORANGE JUICE CONCENTRATE
1 cup NONFAT PLAIN YOGURT or BUTTERMILK
1/2 cup chopped, roasted and peeled NEW MEXICO
     GREEN CHILES, well drained
1 1/2 cups chopped WALNUTS

Syrup:
   2 Tbsp. ORANGE JUICE CONCENTRATE
   JUICE of 1 1/2 LEMONS
   1 cup HONEY
   3 Tbsp. RUM or TEQUILA

Preheat the oven to 350 degrees. Grease and flour a Bundt pan.

In a large bowl cream the butter and sugar together. Beat in the eggs one at a time. Stir in the orange and lemon zests. In a small bowl, stir together the flour, baking powder, soda and salt. Beat in the dry ingredients alternately with the yogurt and juice concentrate. Stir in the chiles and nuts. Pour into the prepared Bundt pan. Bake at 350 degrees for 50 minutes to 1 hour until tests done.

Meanwhile, prepare the syrup by boiling the juices and honey over medium heat in a small saucepan for 3 minutes. Cool and stir in the rum or tequila. When the cake has been out of the oven for 5 minutes, invert onto a plate and slowly spoon the syrup over it. Decorate with slivered candied peppers or orange peel.

Yields one large cake.

Sunflower Pie

This is a tasty pie bursting with sunny golden tropical fruits. The green chiles provide just the right amount of spice and heat in this sweet pie. This original creation is sure to become a family favorite.

Two 9-inch PIE CRUSTS rolled out into two 10-inch circles

Filling:
- **3 ripe yet firm MANGOS, peeled, diced**
- **16 ounce can PINEAPPLE, drained and diced**
- **2 BANANAS, peeled, sliced**
- **1/2 cup chopped, roasted and peeled NEW MEXICO GREEN CHILES**
- **3/4 cup SUGAR (plus 2 Tbsp. if the mangos are not sweet)**
- **1 1/2 tsp. grated LIME ZEST**
- **3 Tbsp. LIME JUICE**
- **1 Tbsp. RUM**
- **2 1/2 Tbsp. CORNSTARCH**
- **3/4 tsp. GROUND CINNAMON**
- **1 1/2 Tbsp. BUTTER**

Preheat the oven to 425 degrees. Arrange one of the pie crusts in a 9-inch pie plate. Sprinkle lightly with a tsp. each of additional sugar and flour. In a large bowl toss together all of the filling ingredients except the butter and let it sit for 10 minutes while readying the top crust. Spoon the filling into the bottom crust and dot with small pieces of the butter. Arrange the second crust on top. Trim the pastry edges and pinch to seal them. Sprinkle the top crust with an additional tsp. of sugar. Cut a few slashes through the top crust to allow steam to release while baking. Cover the edges of the pie with foil and bake at 425 degrees for about 40 minutes until hot and bubbly and top crust is golden brown. Check the pie after 30 minutes and lightly cover the entire pie with foil if the crust appears to be sufficiently brown. Cool the pie and serve with ice cream.

Yields one 9-inch pie, serving 6.

Big Jim Jam

Green chile jam is popular throughout the state. Enjoy it plain or with cream cheese on bread, biscuits or flour tortillas. It can be used in cooking or as a condiment whenever a sweetness with a touch of chile flavor and heat is needed. This recipe is unusually flavorful because it uses only meaty Big Jim chiles and doesn't contain pectin used in many recipes. It's vibrant green color is especially pronounced, too.

25 BIG JIM GREEN CHILES, roasted, peeled, finely chopped
4 small LEMONS, quartered and seeded
1 cup CIDER VINEGAR
6 cups SUGAR

Place six half-pint jars and lids in a large pot of water and boil them for 10 minutes. Remove the jars to paper towels to drain upside down.

In a large heavy-bottomed pot, place the Big Jim chiles, lemons and vinegar. Cook for 30 minutes over medium high heat until everything is tender. Remove the lemons, squeezing their juice into the pot. Add the sugar and boil for 15 minutes until the mixture is thickened and just begins to fall off a spoon in a sheet. Pour the jam into the prepared jars and seal. Can be stored in the refrigerator for several months.

Or, for longer shelf storage, process in a water bath for 15 minutes, plus one minute for every 1000 foot altitude elevation.

Yields 6 half-pint jars.

Hot Chocolate Cookie Clusters

Hot chocolate spiced with cinnamon is a favorite treat for all ages on cold winter evenings. It is also the customary beverage for serving with many of our traditional cookies. These clusters are cookies and hot chocolate in one. Served cold, these no-bake sweets have their own bit of "heat."

2 cups SUGAR
1/2 cup MILK
1/2 cup COCOA POWDER
1/2 cup BUTTER
1 Tbsp. NEW MEXICO RED CHILE POWDER
1/8 tsp. CAYENNE
2 tsp. VANILLA
2 tsp. GROUND CINNAMON
1 1/2 cups ROLLED OATS
3/4 cup RAISINS
3/4 cup dry-roasted, skinless, unsalted PEANUTS

In a large heavy saucepan place the sugar, milk, cocoa and butter. Cook over low heat, stirring frequently, until the butter has melted. Continue to simmer gently for about 3 minutes until the mixture is thick and smooth. Remove the pan from the heat and stir in the remaining ingredients. Cool a few minutes. Butter a cookie sheet and drop the slowly thickening mixture by heaping teaspoonful onto the sheet. Place the cookie sheet in the refrigerator for 1 hour until the clusters have set. Place them in an airtight container and store in the refrigerator.

Yields about 3 dozen clusters.

Farolito Cookies

Farolitos are small paper sacks weighted with sand into which small votive candles are placed. On Christmas Eve they line walkways and rooftops throughout the state. The burning candles create a soft warm glow through the sacks. They symbolize each family's welcome to the Christ child into their home and light his way. This truly charming custom is reflected in these cookies filled with their own tiny bit of fire inside.

Outer "sack" crust:
- **1 cup BUTTER**
- **1 cup POWDERED SUGAR**
- **2 tsp. VANILLA**
- **1 large EGG**
- **1 cup CORNMEAL**
- **1 cup WHOLE-WHEAT PASTRY or ALL-PURPOSE FLOUR**

Filling:
- **8 ounces CREAM CHEESE**
- **1 large EGG**
- **1 1/2 tsp. grated LEMON ZEST**
- **1/2 cup POWDERED SUGAR**

Topping:
- **3 - 4 Tbsp. BIG JIM JAM (see page 101)**

First make the crust. In a large bowl, beat the butter, sugar, vanilla and egg until creamy. Stir in the cornmeal and flour. Chill several hours. In another medium bowl, whip the cream cheese, egg, zest, vanilla and sugar until creamy to make the filling. Keep in the refrigerator until needed.

Preheat the oven to 350 degrees. Form the dough into 1-inch balls, press on sides and bottoms of miniature muffin tins to form 48 cups. Place 1 tsp. of the cream cheese filling inside each. Bake at 350 degrees for 15 minutes until golden. Cool 5 minutes and then remove them to a rack to cool. Place 1/2 tsp. of **Big Jim Jam** on top of each. Cool and store them in the refrigerator.

Yields 48 cookies.

Peanut Cookies with Red Chile Crackle

Peanutty and chocolatey cookies with a touch of heat in the red chile sugar coating. While they bake the red sugar cracks, creating an interesting and colorful coating. If you like your cookies chewy, wrap them airtight while they are slightly warm. For crispier versions, let them cool completely before storing. These freeze well, wrapped airtight, if you can resist eating them hot from the oven!

1 cup BUTTER
1 cup freshly ground PEANUT BUTTER
1 cup SUGAR
1 cup packed BROWN SUGAR
2 large EGGS
1 tsp. VANILLA
3 cups WHOLE-WHEAT PASTRY or ALL-PURPOSE FLOUR
1 Tbsp. BAKING SODA
1 cup dry-roasted, skinless, unsalted PEANUTS
1 cup SEMISWEET CHOCOLATE CHIPS
2 Tbsp. NEW MEXICO RED CHILE POWDER
1/4 cup SUGAR
1/4 tsp. CAYENNE

In a large bowl, beat with a mixer the butter, peanut butter and 1 cup each of white and brown sugar until creamy. Beat in the eggs and vanilla. Stir in the flour and soda until well combined. Stir in the peanuts and chocolate chips. Cover the bowl and place it in the refrigerator for one hour.

In a small bowl, stir together the chile powder, 1/4 cup sugar and cayenne. Preheat the oven to 350 degrees. Lightly grease cookie sheets.

Take heaping tablespoons of the dough and roll into balls. Roll each ball in the chile sugar and place on the cookie sheets, allowing 2 inches between the cookies. Bake at 350 degrees for about 12 minutes until they are lightly golden and just set. Leave on the cookie sheet one minute; then remove them with a spatula to a wire rack to cool.

Yields about 5 dozen cookies.

Orange Fire Chocolate Clusters

These are a cross between a cookie and a candy. The rich chocolate binds the granola-like base. The chile heat is sweetened by the perfume of oranges. These scrumptious bites will keep for a week in the refrigerator.

2 cups SUGAR
1/2 cup MILK
1/2 cup COCOA POWDER
1/2 cup BUTTER
1 Tbsp. NEW MEXICO RED CHILE POWDER
1/8 tsp. CAYENNE
1 tsp. VANILLA
1 2/3 cups ROLLED OATS
3/4 cup RAISINS
3/4 cup dry-roasted, skinless, unsalted PEANUTS
1 1/2 Tbsp. ORANGE LIQUEUR
1 Tbsp. ORANGE JUICE CONCENTRATE

In a large heavy saucepan, stir together the sugar, milk, cocoa and butter. Cook over low heat, stirring frequently, until the butter has melted. Continue to gently simmer for about 3 minutes until the mixture is thick and smooth. Remove from heat and stir in the remaining ingredients. Cool a few minutes. Butter a cookie sheet and drop the slowly thickening mixture by heaping teaspoonful onto the sheet. Place it in the refrigerator for 1 hour until the clusters have set. Store in an airtight container in the refrigerator.

Yields about 3 dozen clusters.

Cheesecake with a Kick

*This is a rich and lemony cheesecake with a pleasing bite of green chile flavor. No one will be able to quite put their finger on the secret ingredient that makes this cheesecake so outstanding, but you'll know it's the **Big Jim Jam**.*

Crust:
- 6 Tbsp. UNSALTED BUTTER
- 1 Tbsp. LEMON ZEST
- 1/2 cup SUGAR
- 1 large EGG
- 1 cup WHOLE-WHEAT PASTRY or ALL-PURPOSE FLOUR
- 2/3 cup finely chopped WALNUTS
- 1/4 tsp. SALT

Filling:
- 2 pounds CREAM CHEESE or NEUFCHÂTEL CHEESE
- 1 1/2 Tbsp. LEMON ZEST
- 1 1/2 cups SUGAR
- 4 large EGGS
- 1/2 cup BIG JIM JAM (see page 101)
- 2 tsp. VANILLA

In a medium size bowl place the butter, 1 tablespoon lemon zest and 1/2 cup sugar and beat until creamy. Beat in the egg until incorporated. Stir in the flour, nuts and salt gently. Lightly grease a 9-inch springform pan with removable sides. Spread the dough onto the bottom of the pan. Cover and place in the refrigerator.

Preheat oven to 350 degrees. Bake the crust at 350 degrees for 15 minutes just until it is set and lightly golden. Remove from the oven and cool. Lower the oven temperature to 300 degrees.

In a large bowl place the cream cheese, 1 tablespoon lemon zest and 1 1/2 cups sugar. Beat until creamy. Beat in the 4 eggs, **Big Jim Jam** and vanilla until fluffy. Pour over the crust. Set a 9-inch pan of boiling water on the bottom rack of the oven. Place the springform pan on the top rack and in the center of the oven. Bake at 300 degrees for 1 hour. Cover top loosely with a foil tent if beginning to brown. Lower oven to 275 degrees and continue baking for 45 - 60 minutes until filling just barely jiggles when the pan is moved. Turn off the oven and let the cake cool in the oven for 45 minutes. Chill in the refrigerator for at least 8 hours before serving.

Yields one 9-inch cheesecake (about 8 servings).

Index

About the Author

Sandy Szwarc is an accomplished food writer, having written for over six years for several regional New Mexico newspapers. With more than fifteen years in recipe development, her recipes have received multiple national recognitions. Her articles and award winning recipes have appeared in such publications as *Saveur, Cooking Light, Better Homes and Gardens, New Mexico Magazine, Christian Science Monitor, Washington Post, Dallas Morning News, Bon Appetit, Gourmet, Sunset Magazine, Country Woman, Sally's Place, Albuquerque Journal, Mountain Living Magazine* and *La Cocinita.* She is currently the senior food writer and editor of national food and gardening magazines.

Sandy is a member of the International Association of Culinary Professionals, the Association of Food Journalists, and the Association of Women in Communications.

This cookbook is the culmination of almost eighteen years of living in New Mexico, studying its traditional cuisine from native cooks as well as experimenting and creating contemporary dishes using the local ingredients she loves. ***Real New Mexico Chile—An Insider's Guide to Cooking with Chile*** has received excellent coverage in *New Mexico Magazine* and has been highly recommended by the *Cookbook Collector* and *Midwest Book Reviewer.*

More Cook Books by Golden West Publishers

NEW MEXICO COOK BOOK

Authentic history and foods of New Mexico. Includes chapters on Indian heritage, chile as a way of life, Mesilla Valley, Santa Fe, Albuquerque, Taos and New Wave recipes. By Lynn Nusom.
5 1/2 x 8 1/2—144 pages . . . $5.95

TORTILLA LOVERS COOK BOOK

From tacos to tostadas, enchiladas to nachos, every dish celebrates the tortilla! More than 70 easy to prepare, festive recipes for breakfast, lunch and dinner. Filled with Southwestern flavors! By Bruce Fischer and Bobbie Salts.
5 1/2 x 8 1/2 — 112 pages . . . $6.95

SALSA LOVERS COOK BOOK

More than 180 taste-tempting recipes for salsas that will make every meal a special event! Salsas for salads, appetizers, main dishes, and desserts! Put some salsa in your life! By Susan K. Bollin.
5 1/2 x 8 1/2—128 pages . . . $5.95

CHILI-LOVERS COOK BOOK

Chili cookoff prize-winning recipes and regional favorites! The best of chili cookery, from mild to fiery, with and without beans. Plus a variety of taste-tempting foods made with chile peppers. 200,000 copies in print! By Al and Mildred Fischer.
5 1/2 x 8 1/2—128 pages . . . $5.95

WHOLLY FRIJOLES!
The Whole Bean Cook Book

Features a wide variety of recipes for salads, main dishes, side dishes and desserts with an emphasis on Southwestern style. Pinto, kidney, garbanzo, black, red and navy beans, you'll find recipes for these and many more! Includes cooking tips and fascinating bean trivia! By Shayne Fischer
5 1/2 x 8 1/2—112 pages . . . $6.95

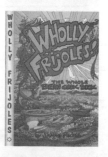

ORDER BLANK

GOLDEN WEST PUBLISHERS

☼ 4113 N. Longview Ave. • Phoenix, AZ 85014

602-265-4392 • **1-800-658-5830** • FAX 602-279-6901

Qty	Title	Price	Amount
	Arizona Cook Book	5.95	
	Best Barbecue Recipes	5.95	
	Chili-Lovers' Cook Book	5.95	
	Chip and Dip Cook Book	5.95	
	Christmas in Arizona Cook Book	8.95	
	Christmas in New Mexico Cook Book	8.95	
	Christmas in Texas Cook Book	8.95	
	Gourmet Gringo Cook Book	14.95	
	Kokopelli's Cook Book	9.95	
	Low Fat Mexican Recipes	6.95	
	Mexican Desserts & Drinks	6.95	
	Mexican Family Favorites	6.95	
	New Mexico Cook Book	5.95	
	Quick-n-Easy Mexican Recipes	5.95	
	Real New Mexico Chile	6.95	
	Salsa Lovers Cook Book	5.95	
	Tequila Cook Book, The	7.95	
	Tortilla Lovers Cook Book	6.95	
	Vegi-Mex: Vegetarian Mexican Recipes	6.95	
	Wholly Frijoles! The Whole Bean Cook Book	6.95	
Shipping & Handling Add ⟹	U.S. & Canada Other countries	$3.00 $5.00	

☐ My Check or Money Order Enclosed $ _____

☐ MasterCard   ☐ VISA ($20 credit card minimum)

_____ (Payable in U.S. funds)

Acct. No.	Exp. Date
Signature	
Name	Telephone
Address	

City/State/Zip
Call for FREE catalog   Real NM Chile

3/98

This order blank may be photo-copied.